GW00771139

lizzie mcgraw

creative Style

liveable, loveable spaces

lizzie mcgraw

creative *Style*
liveable, loveable spaces

Words by Fifi O'Neill
Photography by Mark Lohman

CICO BOOKS
LONDON NEW YORK

Editor: Sophie Devlin
Designer: Louise Leffler
Art director: Sally Powell
Production manager: Gordana Simakovic
Senior commissioning editor: Annabel Morgan
Creative director: Leslie Harrington

Published in 2022 by CICO Books
An imprint of Ryland Peters & Small Ltd
20–21 Jockey's Fields
London WC1R 4BW
and
341 E 116th St
New York, NY 10029
www.rylandpeters.com

10 9 8 7 6 5 4 3 2 1

Text © Lizzie McGraw 2022
Design & photography © CICO Books 2022

The author's moral rights have been asserted. All rights reserved. No part of this publication may be reproduced, stored in a retrieval system, or transmitted in any form or by any means, electronic, mechanical, photocopying, or otherwise, without the prior permission of the publisher.

A CIP catalog record for this book is available from the Library of Congress and the British Library.

ISBN 978 1 80065 163 0

Printed in China

MIX
Paper | Supporting
responsible forestry
FSC® C008047
FSC
www.fsc.org

Contents

Introduction 6

A Merchant in Venice 8

Urban Boho 22

True to Form 36

City Sanctuary 48

A Cottage in California 64

In Perfect Harmony 90

Coastal Vibes 100

Style to Spare 110

Heart and Soul 118

Mediterranean Moments 136

Pacific Paradise 148

Home Couture 160

Above It All 176

Modern Alchemy 190

Index 204   Acknowledgements 208

Introduction

If you've ever tried to recreate a Pinterest DIY project only to have glued your hand to your forehead a few hours later, then this book is for you.

I love seeing women and girls embracing this tool and building their businesses around it. I have seen so much camaraderie and all kinds of ideas being shared. But the truth is that designing the home of your dreams takes a lot more. As a design advisor, it's essential that I find out exactly who you are and how you live. And it takes patience, as I learned when I was rushing an upholsterer to finish a chair for me. His wise response was "It's not an enchilada." I heard him loud and clear—and I have stolen his words when others are pushing me to rush to the finish line. An interior designer is not cheap, but if they're good they'll save you money in many ways. If they're really good, they'll make you laugh and put you at ease along the way. And if they're special, they'll educate you on the difference between making a chair and making an enchilada.

A successful friend of mine recently told me that she had no female mentors, but how can this be? My life is filled with them. From my grandmother to my mother to my first and most amazing boss, Barbra Bryant, I have learned so much from my women friends, bosses and coworkers. Indeed, I wouldn't be where I am today had they not been a part of my life. We are living in a time when women are taking their rightful place in the world, but let's not forget how much has already been achieved. If not for the sacrifices of previous generations of women, we would not be where we are today.

This book is dedicated to every girl who is not sure where she's going, but gets there anyway.

Lizzie McGraw

a merchant in *Venice*

Looking back, it's clear that my love of design and interiors started early on. I was four years old when I decided to paste flowers on my bedroom ceiling so that every night I could look up at a beautiful garden. I got caught—or perhaps rescued—because of the loud noise my bed made when I moved it across the room. When my mother came in and found me, I was standing precariously on a chair, with around 10 books stacked on it, on top of the bed.

I am the daughter of an architect named William J McGraw. The knowledge he instilled in me, both as an artist and as a human being, is immeasurable. Back in 1997, I decided to establish my own store in Venice Beach, California, where I was living at the time. I came to my father and asked for a "loan" to help me get started. He asked me to show him my business plan, and in all sincerity and ignorance I asked, "What's that?" He answered all my questions, and then he gave me a small loan that covered a month's rent. Although I was clueless about starting a business, I always knew that I didn't just want to design spaces—I also wanted to design my life. And so my store, Tumbleweed & Dandelion, was born.

opposite Tumbleweed & Dandelion's unique displays create an easy flow by carrying the eclectic mood from one space to the next. Decorative baskets, books, and shells mingle with more utilitarian items such as tableware and linens. It's a happy mix that results in a harmonious diversity, and contributes to the layered and collected appeal.

above The store has been a mainstay on Abbot Kinney Boulevard in Venice Beach for the past 25 years. It remains a favorite destination for design and decor aficionados.

overleaf Pillows come in a range of patterns and fabrics, accessories run the gamut from laid-back to sophisticated, while furnishings offer a variety of materials and finishes—from raw and rustic to sleek and polished.

Tumbleweed & Dandelion's world is at once joyfully eclectic, sophisticated, collected, laid-back, and filled with personalities that add to our story.

above left Straw hats and baskets come in handy for a day at the beach, which is only a short distance away.

above right Versatile, stylish, and very easy to wrap as presents, these light and softly hued scarves are among our bestselling smaller items.

Since I had no business plan and no real idea of what I was doing, I simply took from my apartment all the street finds that I had restored, put them in my shop, and opened the doors. I remember very clearly the first person to shop with me. She literally bought everything, and I was so nervous I could barely ring up her credit card. Elated and grateful, I then realized the store was empty and I had to hustle for day two! It took many years to establish myself, although lots of people helped along the way. One of my first clients was Julia Roberts, who bought some furniture for her niece Emma. Julia visited many times after that but never knew how much those first sales meant to me.

Tumbleweed & Dandelion is a small shop that I created with the intention of making sure everyone would feel welcome, whether they are spending money or not, and that sentiment carries over into my interior-design process as well. Through our doors walk people of very little means and people with enough cash to buy the entire street, and yet we have found a way to accommodate everyone.

above left Various collections of pillows made from dreamy textiles sourced from all over the world show off rich colors, intricate details, and cultural elements.

above right We make our own fragrant candles—seen here is our very popular Stinky Dog collection.

above Traditional Bhujodi throws are handwoven by artisans in northern India from organic, handspun wool and natural dyes, making each one a unique find. They are sought after for their vivid colors, complex textural details, artisanal quality, nomadic heritage, ethnic vibes, and worldly appeal.

opposite Accessories are not limited to pillows and baskets, though they are among our staples. Carvings, terracotta pottery, and cache pots come in varying sizes, materials, and finishes. Interiors and travel books and French-inspired items keep the mix lively and ever-changing.

left Though the shop isn't large, it's divided into rooms, which makes it easier for us to stage the different spaces in ways that help customers visualize how furniture, accessories, and color combinations can work in their own homes. This living-room display includes chairs upholstered in neutral fabric with a subtle pattern and varied textiles with different tonalities of blue. It demonstrates perfectly how to create a breezy coastal vibe.

above An exquisite but sturdy vintage indigo batik fabric brings unique beauty to this practical ottoman.

left Outdoor rugs come in a wide variety of colors and patterns and are ideally suited to a multitude of alfresco decorating styles, from cottage to boho.

opposite Whether on seat pads, plump pillows, or rugs, striped textiles are always a good fit for a patio or garden. Custom benches and a handsome picnic table spell outdoor living at its coziest. For a touch of drama, we have added a cluster of glossy black urns.

The building on Abbot Kinney Boulevard in Venice Beach that was once my home now houses my store. It is the epicenter of my business where for over two decades we've been designing and handcrafting unique pieces. A lot has changed since the early years, when this area of Venice was notorious for being rather bleak. But now on any given afternoon you can find resident hipsters, well-known designers, artists, musicians, and tastemakers walking along the boulevard, which boasts some of the coolest shops and trendiest eateries in town. By 2012, *GQ* magazine had dubbed it "The Coolest Block in America."

Tumbleweed & Dandelion began its life as a "painted furniture" store, but it now encompasses a line of custom-made furniture and a series of high-end interior-design projects, as well as remaining a shopping destination.

As a manufacturer, we create most of our products in downtown Los Angeles, and we take pride in the fact that we design, make, and sell American-crafted wares.

I have had the honor of designing many different styles of home—beach houses, guesthouses, restaurants, mansions... you name it and we've designed it. From New York City to Los Angeles, I've had the pleasure of working with all kinds of people. The aesthetic may vary, but in our hearts we all just want to feel comfort in our dwellings.

Though our business has grown since our modest beginnings, our principles remain the same: To live our lives with our feet in the sand and our hearts in our work. Tumbleweed & Dandelion's world is at once joyfully eclectic, sophisticated, collected, laid-back, and filled with personalities that add to our story.

opposite Decorating a shop area, like this bedroom space, is similar to furnishing a real home but without some of the practical restrictions. That creative freedom allows for a quick change of furnishings and accessories when new items come in—or whenever the mood strikes.

above Showcasing a piece by making it a focal point helps customers to get the full impact. This antique loveseat with carved wooden legs has been updated with an indigo-and-white block-printed fabric complete with nailhead detailing. It's a meeting of old and new in the best of ways!

urban *boho*

I first met Isabelle Davis when she was 14 years old. She is the daughter of two of my oldest friends and clients, Vicki Gordon and Michael Rubin, whose New York home is featured elsewhere in this book (see "City Sanctuary"). I watched her grow up, but even as a teenager she was wise beyond her years. She's a girl who can handle anything—including one memorable occasion when I fell down her stairs with a glass of red wine, which made it necessary to repaint the staircase.

When Isabelle asked me to help decorate the historic Boston townhouse that she and her husband Stephen had purchased, I was honored. They both already loved the location and the style of the house, which is four stories high with a footprint of 3,500 square feet/325 square meters. For Isabelle, it's similar to the Manhattan brownstone where she grew up, right down to being across the street from a school. The home had been renovated but needed personal touches, built-ins, and, most importantly, an infusion of the couple's "surfer-meets-city-girl" signature style. The goal was to create a space that they both would enjoy spending time in, so the interiors needed to be functional, accessible, comfortable, and stylish.

opposite Grown-up pastels infuse the living room with a youthful vibe, a feeling accentuated by the French painting of a young girl and the modernity of the coffee table. The scheme embraces the interplay of furnishings with straight lines, fluid forms, rounded edges, and clean angles that team up to create softness and sophistication. The handmade rug underscores the eclectic mix.

above The new sofa unites comfort and style. Moroccan silk pillows in faded pink and aqua bring in a global accent and a touch of vintage with their subtle patterns and textures.

We embarked on the project just before the pandemic began and managed to complete a few things during lockdown, even though I was 3,000 miles away. I went into this thinking it was going to be so much fun and with such love for both of them. Little did I know that Covid-19 would close my store for seven months. Unlike interior design, real estate was considered an essential service, so I managed to keep my business alive by staging houses for sale with a small crew of four people. Meanwhile, I was also trying to handle the complexities of Isabelle and Stephen's new home in Boston. I now understand that it's easy to start something but it can be hard to finish it. The evolution of a creative mind isn't something to be ignored, but it's rarely something you are consciously aware of while it is happening. I'm happy that, in hindsight, I'm at least able to pinpoint the beginning of it in my mind.

above The living room is a perfect example of "opposites attract." Rather than conflicting, the curves of the sofa and the straighter lines of the sleek mid-century wooden chairs balance each other, as do their soft white bouclé and brown, buttery leather upholstery. The unexpected addition of a paper pendant light designed by Isamu Noguchi brings the intricate original moldings and ceiling medallion into the present day.

opposite A colorful print of a cassette tape by the French photographer Julien Roubinet adds a whimsical note and makes a great partner for the entryway credenza/sideboard, which has an effortless flair thanks to its clean lines, organic mango-wood frame, and airy handwoven cane door panels.

"Lizzie has a gift for making you feel empowered in your decisions. Her creativity and energy are boundless, and her heart is even bigger than her smile." –Isabelle Davis

left The family room is all
about laid-back modern
bohemian chic with the
"surfer-meets-city-girl" vibe
that the couple wanted. The
juxtaposition of furniture
with curved and straight
lines is an echo of the living
room. Rounded chairs and
tables are combined with
an ample yet streamlined
sofa and a floor lamp with an
angular shade. Texture also
comes into play through the
layering of a hemp rug set
atop a sisal one, the bouclé
chairs, the hand-carved
bleached alder-wood coffee
tables, and the surfboard
mounted on the wall.

above In the eating area, a banquette and airy cane-backed chairs surround a Tulip-style table based on Eero Saarinen's iconic design. Though there is no physical separation between this space and the kitchen, the arrangement creates an intimate setting. The fireplace nearby has been repurposed as a doghouse.

left This contemporary artwork complements the smooth, white marble of the fireplace beautifully.

opposite A custom-built cabinet and shelves are today's version of the classic hutch/dresser. The mugs and bowls introduce bright colors.

Isabelle and Stephen's goal was to preserve the building's original features while instilling a contemporary feel through furnishings, colors, patterns, house plants, and eclectic accessories. They wanted the interior to have a cool, classy, and laid-back style, which we would achieve by uniting modern elements with bohemian chic. The couple are both creative and strong-willed, so deciding what was important to them was a highly collaborative process. They really cared about each other's needs and both were instrumental in making decisions for their home.

They had already done a lot of the work before I got involved, so my role was to figure out what was needed to complete the project and to help with additional furniture details and style decisions. As a group we had many ideas, not all of which were implemented, but we were all delighted with the end result. For instance, I suggested window treatments in designer fabrics, but Isabelle and Stephen decided to go in another direction. Isabelle and I looked at and pulled lots of fabrics and designs that she loved, and then we played. The initial selection was then edited down when Stephen gave his input. In the end, I was just a guide for what works for them. I believe you want your clients to find themselves as opposed to dictating their style. In this case, Isabelle and Stephen

above The kitchen harnesses the natural light to coax a sense of spatial expansiveness and fluidity. A curated palette of materials captures the essence of modernity and practicality. The island's stone countertop and a pair of sizeable pendants unite robustness with refinement. Glass-fronted white cabinetry and white oak flooring underscore the sophisticated-meets-functional approach that defines the space. With all amenities within easy reach, the kitchen performs equally well for simple meals at home or for entertaining family and friends.

have an acute sense of style that made a good amount of the decisions easy. It was so much fun to watch the two of them work together and create a style for their home that is uniquely theirs. Although they can afford to buy most of the things they want, they are both discerning and environmentally conscious —they don't buy just to buy. I have learned a lot from our business relationship. I believe design is something to be planned, but I also think happy mistakes should be welcomed along the way and that using what you have is both more sustainable and less stressful.

Isabelle has a great eye and has brought together a mix of high-end and more affordable pieces that translates into a graceful, dynamic, liveable, and family-friendly interior. For example, in the living room she opted for an iconic handmade rug by Madeline Weinrib, reupholstered mid-century chairs, and an on-trend CB2-style sofa. Stephen's main request was the very comfortable Eames chair in the adjoining family room. When all is said and done, the youthful color palette, furnishings, materials, accessories, and keen eye for art all came together to create a vibrant, joyful home. Isabelle and Stephen are young, but their vision makes a definite grown-up statement and is a manifestation of Isabelle's exquisite sense of design.

above left Isabelle is a food aficionado, so cookbooks are much more than props, though they do make tempting decorative objects with their colorful covers.

above right The graphic stone backsplash complements the sleek stainless-steel appliances and countertop, while the antique breadboard and wooden stool convey a warm touch that tempers the cool, shiny metal.

Because of the pandemic, my team and I faced limitations on what we could order and also what we could make and transport to Boston from our store and warehouse on the West Coast. However, in spite of these restrictions, I am proud to say that Tumbleweed & Dandelion was able to supply a great number of tribal rugs, the numerous hemp pillows, the coffee tables, and many unique and interesting accessories.

In the family room, we installed custom-made floating shelves to open up the space. I can honestly say I make very few design mistakes. I do a lot of things wrong in life, but mostly I measure right. On this particular occasion, though, I somehow wrote down the wrong measurement. I am still (a year later) in disbelief over this, and even though I swiftly replaced the shelves, you never forget the thing that should have been so easy that you fudged up.

opposite A low-hanging rattan pendant, one of a pair in this bedroom, echoes the playful geometric lines of the wall covering—itself a work of art. A sculptural cactus and an unusual crystal on the nightstand add further dimension and intrigue.

above The soothing color scheme and soft, plush textures signal calm and serenity. A multitude of pillows in varied patterns but similar tones and textures keeps the look consistent. Gently rumpled, lived-in bed linen amps up the comfort level. The Mongolian sheepskin pillow and textural rug enhance the *hygge* factor. Together with the airy rattan pendants and curvy African basket, they also keep the overall look current. Bleached pine tables bring a vintage touch and maintain the softness of the palette.

Isabelle has a great eye and has brought together
a mix of high-end and more affordable
pieces that translates into a graceful,
dynamic, liveable, and family-friendly interior.

The home's aesthetic is fresh and youthful with a design consistency from room to room that stems from the juxtaposition of classic and nomadic elements. That intriguing mix of mid-century pieces with plant life and bohemian bits is quite lovely! I can see the couple taking a few things from this house with them as they grow into their next home because the overall look offers a timeless, comfortable chic, and the biggest thing you can't teach is effortless style. Their home has the grace of Isabelle's mother Vicki, reinterpreted in her own unique way. The house feels both ageless and ethereal to me.

I love when design transcends any label, and I think this home does just that.

opposite left Comfort doesn't mean forgoing style. Isabelle opted for a soft chair in the nursery, where she can cuddle with her baby girl, and a rattan table to hold varied items as needed.

opposite right The stylishly simple dresser/chest of drawers with its tactile leather handles doubles up as a changing table. The drawer pulls match the leather brackets of the pair of small wooden shelves on the wall above.

above The practical work of creating a safe, comfortable, beautiful, serene room for a baby is unique to that space. Isabelle designed the wallpaper herself and chose a crib with a little touch of mid-century style. The deep-pile flokati rug provides comfort underfoot, while the custom daybed invites both naps and playtime.

true to *form*

Sometimes life's happenings are all about kismet. I once staged a house for sale on behalf of a client and the buyer purchased everything in the home because she felt it had all been curated so well. In fact, she was so impressed that she then invited me to come and meet her in person. As I pulled up to the house for the meeting, her realtor, who was just leaving, said to me: "Write down this number." I did, and she insisted: "Call him; you will thank me." The number belonged to Dan Stern, and I am so thankful to that realtor because Dan and his wife Nanna are truly special people. They are successful, but they are also very kind and creative. Working for them and with them is a designer's dream.

Dan and Nanna live primarily in New York, so this home in Santa Monica, California is a place for their older children to enjoy when they are home from college, and a guest retreat for friends—it's frequently occupied by a friend of a friend of a friend who needs a favor. As Dan says: "The idea was to create an interior that had to be accessible to everyone, reflective of the mid-century roots of the house, and fun!" That sums up how great Dan and Nanna are.

opposite Painting the bricks of the fireplace white has heightened the feeling of airiness in the living room. The sunburst mirror, which was a very popular decorative feature in the 1970s when the house was built, reflects the light, softens the brickwork, and adds a touch of glamour and a dash of drama. A set of drums implies fun days ahead.

above Despite being from different parts of the world, a painting bought at a French flea market and a vintage American radio pair up perfectly.

below A photograph of
swaying palm trees against
a turquoise sky and a
whimsical lamp fashioned
from a textural tree stump
make an artistic statement
on the beauty of nature.

"Our favorite room is the living room.
It's completely mid-century in its feeling,
totally comfortable, and still elegant.
When our friends stay in the house,
they never want to leave! (which is exactly what we want!)"—Dan Stern

Poised on a hill over looking the Pacific Ocean, the 1970s ranch-style house boasts an open floor plan and large windows that bring the indoor and outdoor living spaces into harmony with each other and encourage integration with nature. It made sense to go with a palette that would take advantage of the architecture and complement the surrounding nature and the views. The soft yellows, blues, and pinks of the sunset and the indigo waters of the ocean were the obvious choices.

above Unhindered by curtains, wall-to-wall windows and glass doors invite the sculptural garden to become part of the living-room decor. Generous, low-profile sofas, layered with an assortment of pillows with globally influenced patterns, surround the Isamu Noguchi coffee table to form an engaging conversation area anchored by a Moroccan rug with a nomadic pattern. We specifically selected furniture that would not interfere with the view and the light, like the pair of custom chairs. Taller elements, such as plants and the shapely floor lamp, act as a frame for the landscape beyond.

above The living room is open to the dining area and the kitchen beyond with the same poplar flooring running throughout. The new table's simple lines and glass top and the open backs of the vintage chairs maintain the visual flow that characterizes the living room. Keeping the kitchen sink and most of the cabinetry in a narrow, galley-like area allows the island and shelves, stocked with plates and cooking staples, to become one with the dining room.

right The wall-mounted stainless-steel shelf has an industrial vibe, while the gray metal cabinet below features a quartz work surface.

opposite The mid-century credenza/sideboard, the sleek Isamu Noguchi pendant, and the vintage rug are in harmony with the newer table. Glass panels allow a hazy view of the rock garden and plants in the home's entrance.

Dan and Nanna are knowledgeable, intuitive, and fair, and they were very receptive to our ideas—since the project had to be completed in just two months, they were willing to let us roll. By then, we had a clear vision of what needed to be accomplished. We designed the house to be practical and beautiful, thus giving us an opportunity to flex our creative skills in an authentic way while heeding Dan's design requests for the interior "to honor the home's roots but also be fun."

The moment you enter the house, it's evident that mid-century modern style rules this roost. Though pared down, the aesthetic that unites the interiors is full of warmth and contributes to the relaxed atmosphere. Devoid of excess ornamentation, new and vintage pieces with minimalist silhouettes and natural shapes, such as the iconic Isamu Noguchi coffee table and the kitchen ceiling pendant, are as beautiful in their simplicity as they are functional.

above The view of the surrounding bamboos gives the guest bedroom the impression of being in a tree house. Simply but stylishly furnished, the room strikes an easygoing chord. The warm wooden furniture and rich blue accents dial up the color palette. A vintage map of Santa Monica ties home and location together.

opposite This useful niche hosts custom shelves and a slab of wood that acts as a desk. A vintage chair and an ottoman upholstered in mudcloth bring additional color and pattern to an already upbeat space.

The soft colors from the furnishings and the pale poplar floor add to the luminous quality of the home's interior and engender its restful mood. However, we also made sure to include the hints of playfulness that Dan and Nanna had requested. For instance, we introduced a slightly bohemian feel with unique vintage rugs, touchable textiles, one-of-a-kind art and objects, and a profusion of plants.

These characterful touches soften the clean lines of the furniture and complement the prevailing style rather than clashing with it. Although we stayed faithful to the spirit of the mid-century architecture, adding these elements allowed us to bring in the fun factor. In the process, we created a home that not only yields a wealth of aesthetic rewards but also reflects Dan and Nanna's personal style.

Maybe it is a combination of the wonderful flow of light, colors, materials, and textures that extends from the interiors to the patio and the exceptional succulent gardens, but there is something truly magical about this home. Everyone who spends any time here can feel it as soon as they step inside.

In addition to all the above qualities, I think the magic of this home is best described as, quite simply, a manifestation of Dan and Nanna's kindness, their gracious hospitality, and, ultimately, their discerning tastes.

left The master bedroom's mid-century nightstands and bench are a match for the modern comfort of the upholstered bed. A vintage rug and a Moroccan pouffe add a touch of boho flair to the cocoon-like palette of creams, grays, and warm browns. Leather, wood, and fabrics elevate the visual and tactile appeal.

right We updated the original powder room with a marble vanity and tiles and a stone floor, but included a small vintage rug for good measure.

right Shape and color often come together in surprising ways and prove to be the perfect companions.

overleaf Step out from either the living room, dining room, kitchen, or master bedroom and you will enter a dreamy courtyard that backs onto a unique, self-sustaining succulent garden. With multiple outdoor views and access points, this house embodies the mid-century design principle that a home should exist as part of its environment rather than an imposition on the natural order of things.

city *sanctuary*

Around 15 years ago, a powerful, beautiful woman walked into my store, fell in love with my wall painting, and exclaimed: "If this girl lived in New York City, I'd hire her in a heartbeat." Connie, one of my sales associates, replied: "You're in luck—she's in Manhattan right now."

Connie is a discerning judge of character and taste—she has a gift for identifying serious buyers—and she felt this was a connection I should make. She rang me in New York with the very firm advice to "make the call," so I did, right away. At the time, the name Vicki Gordon meant nothing to me, but I was quick to realize her nearly impenetrable importance when her assistant answered the phone and said Vicki would call me back. She didn't.

The second time I called, I was fortunate enough to get through to Vicki, but it turned out that the brief exchange was due to my voice sounding similar to her daughter Isabelle's. When she realized her mistake she abruptly said, "I'll call you back." She didn't. But I didn't let that discourage me. The evening before I was to leave New York, I phoned one final time, just to say I was sorry I had missed her and that she should stop by the next time she was in Los Angeles.

opposite While furnishing a new-build home with a modern aesthetic is easy, it was trickier in this historic Manhattan brownstone. A pillow and a couple of throws inject a bit of color into the neutral palette. The gilded mirror was found at an antiques show, while the painting is a family heirloom. The coffee and side tables were chosen for their glass tops, which bring a modern note to the space.

above Textural elements—including an antique ceramic jar repurposed as a planter—come together in an organic vignette on a wicker tray.

Would you believe it, this time the once elusive Mrs Gordon called me back: "What do you mean? You're leaving? We have to meet. Come here in the morning before your flight and we'll chat." During our "chat," I agreed to paint Vicki's home on the Upper West Side, and so our journey began. A journey that, for me, gave the phrase "in over your head" a new meaning.

There is nothing as rewarding than when you form an enduring friendship with a client, as is the case with Vicki and her husband Michael Rubin. Over the years since they moved into their heritage brownstone, the couple's taste had evolved and the time had come to update the interiors. When we met, Vicki was looking to replace the existing hybrid of French country chic and romantic styles and achieve the kind of elegance you would find in the pages of *Elle Decor*, without forsaking the 1880s charm.

In typical New York fashion, the home has buildings on either side and windows only on the front and back, making it the first row/terraced house I had worked on. However, with a large kitchen and living room, four bedrooms, five bathrooms, and a backyard, the place was also the most spacious privately owned New York property I had ever set foot in at the time.

above left Delicate branches of cherry blossom heighten the living room's less-is-more elegance.

left Painting and stenciling floors have long been staples of Tumbleweed & Dandelion's decorative arsenal. Here we painted a faux rug with a soft yellow base and classic pattern, which is in keeping with the historic home's roots.

opposite The living room integrates old and new and textural and sleek elements seamlessly. A large painting that Vicki acquired some 30 years ago, vintage shutters, and woven baskets contribute a European feel, while the Eames lounge chair and glass-topped coffee table provide smart, contemporary touches.

The generous proportions turned out to be as useful as the house was a challenge to refinish. For one thing, I learned that the light in a row/terraced house is incredibly tricky to work with. I never really believed in "different shades of white" until this project. One wall would look pink while the adjacent wall (painted in the same color) looked gray and then they would swap depending on the time of day. I also discovered that original plaster moldings from the 19th century have a tendency to fall apart as soon as you touch them. And I found out that a team of hungry painters can eat more in a day than they're being paid in a week, and that people get homesick the most when they're least expecting it. Most importantly of all, I learned to lead.

Vicki is very detail-oriented, doesn't miss a thing, and has her own style. Of course, when your client has style (not always the case), the process can be more difficult when you are in the trenches of decision-making, but it is also far more rewarding in the end. A house like this in NYC is not a dollar and consequently it is not a dollar to fix, furnish, or run. That said, Vicki can make a vintage straw hat over her bed look hip. That is the key.

above Vicki has owned this sofa for many years, but new slipcovers keep it fresh and current. We designed the ottomans, which can easily be moved for additional seating when needed. The soft palette is gently enlivened with touches of color and texture from accessories. Though the overall look is pristine and chic, the room offers substantial comfort and sophistication with an approachable, lived-in feel.

right Original to the 1880s building, the narrow folding shutters have a warm tone that adds authentic charm and balances the modernity of the side table. We designed the armchairs with gently curved backs, which soften the more linear elements.

below Accessories in neutral hues, with occasional pops of color, create a harmonious whole.

"Lizzie is incredibly creative and so easy to work with. We are long past the client stage, we are soulmates."–Vicki Gordon

Vicki is always very kind to credit me with a lot of the work on this house, but in truth I just gave her the confidence to become one with it. And this home is so very Vicki. It brings together all the things that make her happy. The design includes a lot more than just the furniture, rugs, and pillows. It's the fresh flowers she has chosen that week, the candles she's burning, and the table she sets so eloquently.

Most people pick the same things over and over again. If you are a T-shirt-and-jeans person, you don't usually change. I soon lost count of how many magazines Vicki had saved for me so that we could spend hours looking at them, only to find that she had picked out photographs of the same sofa and chair again and again. It certainly helped us solidify what she likes. There is something so gratifying about seeing a wish list of ideas realized.

opposite The brick wall in the kitchen, which was previously bare, is part of the home's heritage. We updated it with a coat of white paint, which has made it a perfect backdrop for Vicki's collection of gleaming copper pots and pans.

above left One of Vicki's favorite features is the fireplace, because it opens on both sides and preserves the connection between the living room and kitchen without interrupting the flow from one space to the other.

above right The pantry was an addition from several years ago, not part of the original layout, but the intricate design of its unique arched window makes it timeless, adds country charm, and ties in with the 19th-century architecture of the rest of the house.

opposite Vicki had the kitchen's original tiny window replaced with a spacious bay window and added the built-in bench to take advantage of the natural light and the garden beyond. It also makes a great place to sit and read by the fire.

left From blowsy to demure, arrangements of softly hued and fragrant fresh flowers are always included in Vicki's decor.

above The kitchen is outfitted with the same traditional-meets-modern theme that runs throughout Vicki and Michael's home. Glass-fronted cabinets, sleek stainless-steel appliances, a marble backsplash, and slipcovered dining chairs speak of up-to-date design yet unite harmoniously with the classic elegance of the table and the graceful lines of the original chandelier overhead.

Bringing the lovingly assembled vision board to life began by creating a soft and pleasing palette throughout the home. When shades easily flow from one space to the next, the effect is tranquil and calming. With that in mind, we kept our colors clean and simple to ensure continuity, as consistency and fluidity were important components of the overall look.

Materials that are pleasing to the touch and pieces that have a natural affinity with the room help to make a space feel like a cohesive whole. However, it's equally important not only to consider aesthetics but also longevity, as well as sourcing ethically and sustainably made products where possible. My mantra has always been "quality over quantity" and the new concept for Vicki and Michael's home has a refreshed aesthetic based on harmonious tones, contemporary flourishes juxtaposed with their vintage treasures, personal mementoes, and cool art. We created spaces with a bit of formality and sophistication that are stylishly comfortable but never stuffy. The refined and contemporary design has produced layered interiors that feel warm and embracing, and are brimming with meaning and atmosphere. Although this is an urban home, when you step inside you feel as though you are in the country—unusual for a Manhattan house with neighbors on both sides.

One of my favorite rooms is the library. It sits at the front of the house and is bathed in beautiful natural light. Both Vicki and Michael used to work in network news, so the television is often switched on elsewhere in their home, but never in this calm space. Being a step away from the endless stream of information is both convenient and peaceful, but what really distinguishes this room and makes it so endearing is the array of personal treasures— including family photographs, items collected from the pair's travels around the world, cherished autographed books, and signed works of art, along with the numerous awards they both garnered from their respective careers in the media.

opposite The narrow hallway leads from the front door to the library, living room, and kitchen. The creamy white walls and stenciled floor runner highlight the staircase and the antique bench nestled in the small recess under the stairs. Vicki bought the colorful painting from a street artist.

above We made the large seat pad and pillow in two fabrics with contrasting textures and styles but with similar hues. Pairing them with the bench illustrates how lovely the union of old and new can be.

above White paint subtly brings the original fireplace and mirror into alignment with the library's new look. A vintage poster from one of Vicki and Michael's trips to the Cannes Film Festival hangs on the wall beside the stately chimneypiece. The Moroccan rug anchors the room with subtle shading and texture.

left Piling logs in the fireplace establishes an inviting and homey feel.

opposite The floor-to-ceiling bookcases hold some of Vicki's extensive book collection and share the spotlight with numerous Emmys and other awards that she and Michael received for the stellar television news programs they produced over many years. Gifts from friends and objects brought back from global treks are both sentimental and meaningful. The bouclé footstool and chairs and Sputnik chandelier add to the sophisticated, *au courant* vibe.

I love this house and I love its people. Vicki and Michael are busy professionals living in New York City, yet they have dinners together in the kitchen with a real fire roaring as the backdrop to lively conversations. They are in touch with each other on a very high level. They have been so welcoming to me for many years that I truly do consider them a part of my family. I am so appreciative and grateful for the opportunity and the love that has come with it.

Casual yet polished, this house has a serene, liveable sensibility with a quiet sophistication and an authentic, intimate vibe. But, ultimately, its innate aura of gravitas is an accurate reflection of its owners. This is a home in every sense of the word. It is, indeed, a peaceful sanctuary in the heart of the city that never sleeps.

below The master bedroom's calm palette makes it feel miles away from Manhattan. In lieu of curtains, small shutters allow for privacy when needed while letting natural light flow in when left open. The stained-glass windows serve as artwork.

opposite left The headboard is covered with a scarf from Thailand. A traditional West African juju hat, symbolizing prosperity, hangs on the wall above. Together, these exotic touches imbue the neutral scheme with personality.

opposite right Heaped with softly hued, comfy pillows, the built-in window seat is a magical spot to dream, read, or savor a cup of coffee.

This home is so very Vicki. It brings together all the things that make her happy. The design includes a lot more than just the furniture, rugs, and pillows. It's the fresh flowers she has chosen that week and the table she sets so eloquently.

a cottage in California

In 2004, I happened to be driving down a tree-lined street in the Inglewood area of Los Angeles and I noticed a woman putting up a For Sale sign in front of a small and ramshackle old cottage. I knew straight away that it was my house. I asked my partner Jonathan to come and see it with me, but when I gave him the address he said, "I am not living in that neighborhood." Nonetheless, I insisted that he please take a look at it with me.

Mind you, we had lost our lease at our old retail location in 2001, so five of our friends had helped us to move into our shop on Abbot Kinney Boulevard in Venice Beach. We also had a dog and two cats. How Jonathan and I managed to stay together with that crew for three years while keeping the store open seven days a week, I will never know. Let's say it was pure determination—and a touch of desperation as well. I will forever remember the time when Jonathan forgot to lock the door and some customers came in while I was in the bathtub. I had to explain my situation and ask them to leave and lock the door behind them. Although I was designing homes for others, I had not yet found my own.

opposite The front porch is one of my favorite spots. It sets the tone for the cottage and is such a cozy little nook for reading, making phone calls, or just catching my breath. It's simply furnished with flea-market finds. Other than watering the plants and giving the floor a new coat of paint from time to time, it requires minimal upkeep. I love its charming old-school look.

above A new seat pad and a heap of pillows in assorted patterns bring new life and comfort to an old wicker sofa.

above When you work with a neutral palette and beautiful materials, they speak for themselves—you don't need a lot of color. White is timeless and understated, so it is always in style. I like to unite European influences, represented here by an antique armoire, with contemporary pieces.

far left Vintage pieces, such as this weathered trunk and rattan lamp, add charm and authenticity.

left Snowy, airy cherry blossoms have a delicate beauty that I love.

opposite We designed the sofa and coffee table ourselves, but the pendant light and portraits came from flea markets in and around Paris. The small cabinet under the painting is a vintage record player. I love when a variety of whites comes together in a space, whether in the paint, furnishings, fabrics, or materials—any and all of it.

When we finally went to view our prospective new home, I asked Jonathan not to say anything and to keep an open mind. The house, which was really little more than a shack, had original Thomas Edison wiring (seriously!) and some of its internal walls had been removed. All the rooms had fluorescent ceiling lights. Need I go on? However, when the owner showed us the guesthouse, Jonathan said: "We'll take it!" It was another shell of a building located at the back of the main house, but even he could see that it had great potential. Thankfully, the property was affordable and we knew (sort of) how to fix things, so it became our new project.

My late father, the architect William J McGraw, was instrumental in the renovation of the house and guesthouse during those first few years. However, it has been a long journey, which is still in progress as I find things to redo every year. Making time to work on your own house is always challenging when you are working on clients' homes non-stop, but we continue to improve and reinvent the cottage, one thing at a time. Recently, because I didn't have the time for a full remodel, I vaulted the ceilings of the living room and kitchen. It has made a huge difference to the space and it's a decision that I'm confident I will not regret in the future.

above These rustic, artisanal double peg racks not only have an artistic and organic presence but they also serve multiple functions, from displaying plants to storing hats. The natural finish of the wood echoes the honey tones of the other pieces.

opposite The dining area is open to the living room. Despite the small size of the space, the first impressions are of light, loftiness, and simplicity thanks to the white walls and high wooden ceiling. The elegant Tulip table, inviting chairs, and organic accessories carry the decor theme from one space to the next, resulting in an uncluttered cohesiveness.

Good design involves showcasing what you love
and eliminating what doesn't serve you.

above The den is our casual spot where we can kick back and relax with our three dogs. I like that the floor shows wear and tear and that the sofa's slipcovers have seen many washes. This room is also home to unique vintage pieces, such as the drum table, which is a prop from a Shirley Temple movie, the "Welcome Firemen" flag, and the old wicker table.

opposite Though compact, the kitchen offers all the necessary amenities and its high shelves provide ample storage. Teaming nostalgic items, such as the O'Keefe and Merritt stove, with newer items keeps the space classic yet current. The pops of red liven up the decor, while the baskets, light pendants, and rug add warmth and texture.

Every home has its own mood. I have always thought of mine as an evening home, especially when the fire pit is roaring and all the candles are lit. That said, lately I have come to realize how beautiful the interiors are on a very sunny day. This has led me to decide that when the time comes for our next remodel, the room that is currently our bedroom will become an office so that we can take advantage of the natural light.

Though my home has evolved over the years, I think what I love today is what I have always loved. What has changed is how I use what I love. For instance, I've saved a smock of my grandmother's for many years because it reminds me of her. She'd be thrilled to know it's now a pillow... or maybe not, but regardless, it's now a pillow. I have always felt most comfortable in interiors that have a calm palette, yet what I desire more now is not just a soothing environment but a simple one as well. I know that will change again in the future, because our homes represent the time of life we are in, but I am leaning into that.

opposite The small hallway leading to the bedroom can be seen from the living room, so it has to be pleasing. It's just large enough to accommodate a favorite timeworn cabinet and a few family heirlooms. Incorporating things you love and appreciate makes your home feel intentional and welcoming.

above left Some things are priceless—this wicker chair came from my mother and the blue-painted shutters from my father.

above right I enjoy styling vignettes and the top of the cabinet offers a perfect stage for my displays, which change depending on the time of year.

above Less isn't always more, especially when it comes to collections. Displaying a grouping of like-colored bottles in different shapes and sizes makes a delightful decorative statement.

right Pairing fresh roses with those on the lamp and the peeling finish of the nightstand imparts a sweet, romantic touch.

opposite The whitewashed, wood-beamed ceiling, wide floor planks, and tongue-and-groove and beadboard walls of our bedroom are quintessential cottage features. It's a serene, restful space with minimal furnishing. Recycled pieces like the table lamps and nightstand honor the cottage's vernacular and are eco friendly, which are two imporant values for me. A few aqua and earthy accents add warmth to the crisp white scheme.

I truly believe in the art of recycling. Not only is it good for the environment but I've also found more treasures at the local flea market than I ever could at a corporate home goods store. Furnishing your home, your life, and your soul takes a great deal of creativity and self-awareness. The best way to become one with your sanctuary is to understand who you are. For instance, I love any and all styles of decorating, which can be problematic when it comes to making decisions. However, compromise is a critical part of building a home and it's necessary to understand what works best for all. My number one rule is follow your heart, not the latest trends—or as my father always said: "Never force anything, other than mayonnaise lids." These words of wisdom can apply to many circumstances, but are certainly fitting when it comes to design.

above The dining room needed to be informal yet welcoming. The recipe to achieve the look came from stirring together texture and patina, repurposed and found objects, and vintage pieces. Uniting the credenza/sideboard with the garden furniture and keeping the finishes to a simple palette of natural wood and painted surfaces also contribute elegance and rustic chic. I love an abundance of fresh flowers and greenery in an eclectic array of containers. It's like having an indoor garden.

opposite There is something inherently beguiling about pieces from the past. Whenever you marry their charms with utilitarian items, you end up with a winning combination. The wooden sign, the pair of shapely finials, and the ceramic roosters impart an ageless beauty, while the simple dishes and crockery convey practicality. Texture, tone, and a blend of organic materials and natural colors bring the display to life.

I've saved a smock of my grandmother's
for many years because it reminds me of her.
She'd be thrilled to know it's now a pillow...
or maybe not, but regardless, it's now a pillow.

I like utilizing what I have and displaying older pieces alongside newer items for various reasons. These possessions have immense sentimental value and I am still happy with them. I am modern, but not modern enough to live sparsely. Our home's heartfelt and homey mood stems from an easy balance of casual furnishings, unique accents, and vintage pieces.

Personality in the items you choose and the way you live is also an important factor in creating spaces that are a reflection of you. Nowadays I feel the need to include art of all kinds in my designs because I find such joy in the creativity of others. The world has gotten so small that artistic cultures are vanishing. When I find bits of history, I always try to incorporate them into my interiors.

I need my home to be a serene setting with a quiet energy, which is why I like to surround myself with lots of architectural and design books for reference, reminders, and inspiration. I also like to have great authors on my shelves and music playing in the background—these things give me the enthusiasm to be creative and express myself.

opposite The California lifestyle encourages outdoor living. Our kitchen opens onto an intimate courtyard, so we can often enjoy alfresco meals. The space is set up similar to what you often find on the terraces of restaurants in villages in the French countryside: simple furnishings like the utilitarian table, an old bench with pillows for added comfort, and candles ready to imbue the setting with a sense of romance at nighttime.

above right For a casual vibe, the courtyard is outfitted with a spacious built-in sofa layered with blue-and-white pillows, plus occasional tables.

right Creating a centerpiece that evokes nature is easily achieved by grouping old green glass bottles in a rustic wooden tray.

The best way to become one with your sanctuary

is to understand who you are.

above left Jonathan and I love to welcome our friends and family. Because the cottage itself is rather small, we have set up a spacious entertaining area on the terrace between the lower and upper levels of the property. It's furnished with vintage wicker chairs, sturdy tables, and sofas designed to accommodate large parties. Statement pieces like the mirrored doors, shutters, urns, and wrought-iron arch add just enough drama.

above right I love using pillows en masse because they instantly cozy up any space. I like to keep them in the same color family but vary the sizes, fabrics, and patterns.

opposite Like the cottage, the guesthouse had to undergo a major renovation. Still, we have endeavored to keep as many original features as possible, such as the kitchen's ceiling and open rafters. This space has a gently rustic feel thanks to the artisanal beauty of handmade pieces and the softness of their wood tones. The tiled wall keeps the look simple while setting off the row of pottery and the uncontrived display of items that we use on a daily basis.

above Hunting for one-of-a-kind items at flea markets is always thrilling, especially when you find something like this wire basket!

Nurture and nature go hand in hand, and to that end, including greenery to bring life and beauty into rooms is a must. There are obvious benefits to surrounding and filling your home with plant life—after all, the endorphins are high when your plant game is strong. Communicating with nature and integrating it in your interiors is paramount in establishing a well-balanced design.

My home is a laboratory where I can experiment by bringing in something from our new homeware collections at Tumbleweed & Dandelion or from our warehouse. It's a great way to open a discussion with anyone who comes to visit, but it also often leads to new design direction and even transformations, such as reupholstering a chair with a rug or making an old sweater into a pillow. Everything we create has evolved out of relationships and needs. For instance, in the beginning my first business partner and I made our own pillows to sell in the store, but at some point along the way I realized that we needed a more skillful maker, which led us to our fabulous seamstress.

Our range of candles started because we wanted to create something that represented our brand, and our furniture has been a wonderful collaboration with two small bespoke workrooms.

If Jonathan had his way, our home would look like a warehouse with three pieces of furniture. Unfortunately for him, he lives with me, so our world is white and tranquil. This gentle palette not only helps me deal with the hustle and bustle inherent to the design world but also with the menagerie of pets that lives here with us. We currently have three big dogs, all mixed breeds: Tripper, Rocky, and Piper. We have a history of taking in animals that have been abused or have serious health issues. For instance, we found Piper when she was left chained to the gate of the Tumbleweed & Dandelion warehouse when she was still a puppy. I think the people who left her there must have heard about my reputation as an animal lover, so they knew she would be in safe hands. The way the property is laid out means our pets have plenty of room to roam, as well as being conducive to setting up inviting garden destinations.

opposite At an exclusive sale of items from Gore Vidal's private collection, I acquired this French 18th-century screen with hand-painted bucolic motifs. It now occupies a place of honor in the guesthouse.

above The guesthouse's main living area includes the living room, dining room, and kitchen, so maintaining a cohesive look was a must. A neutral palette of whites and earth tones and the pairing of antique items like the living room vintage sign and the wood panels with current furniture helped to connect the spaces to each other.

The outdoor concept was designed to promote an alfresco lifestyle and to take advantage of the spaces on offer from the ground up. The cottage sits at the bottom of the hill and opens onto a brick courtyard backing up on an ivy-draped retaining wall. We enjoy this intimate and casual spot daily for morning coffee and evening meals, so it was important to keep it simply but comfortably furnished. From there, steps fashioned with old bricks and rustic wooden boards meander through flowering shrubs to the next level. Here, a large stone terrace cradled by mature trees sets the perfect stage for entertaining with sturdy yet stylish weather-friendly chairs, sofas, and an ample dining table, while above it the guesthouse deck welcomes with colorful cottage-style pieces and offers a spot of choice for stargazing and watching the sunrise.

We love our small cottage, its garden "rooms," and the indoor-outdoor lifestyle. When we are at home together, we truly enjoy ourselves. Style is a very personal thing and your home should be about what makes you feel content. Don't aim for perfection, aim for serenity. It's what I hope all our clients feel when their home is done.

above left With brighter hues and globally inspired textiles, the guesthouse bedroom has a low-key boho vibe. A pair of vintage doors repurposed as a headboard and baskets hanging on the wall maintain the cottage feel. To ensure guests' comfort, the queen-size bed was a must. However, with space at a premium a compromise was needed, hence the small stools that serve as nightstands.

above right The artistic designs of these indigo-blue batik pillows contribute an exotic touch to the bed.

opposite There's just something utterly welcoming and comforting about an antique fireplace, even a non-functioning example like the one in this spacious bathroom. Not only does it evoke feelings of warmth and comfort but it also acts as a focal point.

left The deck gets its cheerful mood from classic Adirondack chairs painted aqua and from the similar hue of the wood planks, which were stenciled by Tumbleweed & Dandelion's master painter Eloy Hernandez. The rug, coffee table, little cabinet, and striped pillows round out the cottage vibe.

left Whether inside or out, plants are an integral part of organic, biophilic design.

opposite My father William was highly instrumental in my life and career. I cherish every piece I got from him, including these large doors that now stand tall on the guesthouse deck. They make the perfect backdrop for the sitting area. Not only do they add vertical dimension but they also help to create a room-like environment, which is further enhanced by the cozy fire pit.

in perfect *harmony*

One of the many components of my business is the staging of homes for sale. This is a rather involved process that requires having a huge number of pieces of furniture, home accessories, and other props readily available. Fortunately, we have a large warehouse that we keep fully stocked for these types of projects, as well as a talented team of designers who are ready for action at a moment's notice.

Staging has to be accomplished very quickly, so I tend to think of it as "speed-styling." Unlike designing a residential interior, in which you have to consider the particular needs of the people who live there, staging is the preparation of a house for sale. The goal is to help the property appeal to the highest possible number of potential buyers by highlighting all its best features to create interiors that are inviting, warm, and current. In short, it should be an irresistible visual feast.

As fate would have it, it was through one such project that I met Adam Malka. Adam was looking for a property and ended up buying this contemporary home, along with all the furniture. After he moved in, Adam decided he wanted to redo the rooms to be more in tune with his design aesthetic and sensibilities. And so our journey began.

opposite The foyer of Adam Malka's home heralds a harmonious mix of modern sensibility with intriguing cultural accents and organic influences. The graphic design of the open staircase is softened by the inclusion of airy, cascading greenery that, in turn, establishes a sympathetic dialogue with the outdoors. The vintage mid-century loveseat is upholstered in a Chinese blue-and-white fabric. Together with the handwoven Moroccan rug, it exemplifies the fusion of traditional craftsmanship that we aimed to harness throughout this project.

above Batik is an ancient Chinese handicraft method that produces uniquely dyed textiles in various shades of blue, as seen on the bench and its pillow.

Adam is an artist and the co-founder and co-CEO of one of the largest music production companies creating soundtracks for television, film, and online media. He has a joyful spirit and loves to entertain—his aunt Judy can often be found baking banana bread in the kitchen, and he frequently hosts gatherings of friends either indoors or in one of the three main outdoor spaces. In particular, the main terrace is easily accessed from the living room and is outfitted with all the essential amenities for congenial get-togethers.

Cultural, biophilic, and organic design are hallmarks of Adam's personal style, which is evident in the fabrics he chooses and the many green plants that make a tangible connection with nature. The effect is further enhanced by the use of predominantly natural materials and finishes throughout—from wood, stone, and jute to hemp, leather, and rattan.

above The living room, kitchen, and dining room comprise the open-plan living space at ground level. The kitchen has a neutral backdrop consisting of a wooden island and matching cabinetry, with the grain providing textural interest. Barstools done up in mudcloth bring in a splash of color. Sleek white wall cabinets, a lustrous tile backsplash, a pair of clear pendant lights, and stainless-steel appliances add a subtle energy.

above right Besides holding cultural significance in Mali, where it first originated, mudcloth is very strong and durable. These qualities make it an excellent choice for upholstery.

right Made from hand-carved alder wood that has been bleached, these drum-style tables have a simple elegance that contributes to the chic, organic vibe.

left The living room is an ode to biophilic design and to Adam's appreciation for pieces with a cultural heritage. Framed by silky curtains, a bank of windows lets the natural light bathe the room and opens up a view of the lush foliage that surrounds the home. A generous assortment of green plants facilitates a connection between the interior and exterior realms. The Moroccan rug anchors the ample sofa and makes a fitting companion for two ottomans upholstered with hemp rugs. The black fabric of the mid-century chair lends a modern edge.

"Lizzie's work has a timeless,

above We designed the dining-room table and chairs to provide visual continuity from the kitchen and living room and to continue the modern-meets-traditional theme. Though the chairs' upholstery shows subtle variations in both color and pattern, they are united by their blue-and-white palette.

left Rather than unifying the chairs by using identical fabric, we opted to give each pair its own individuality. From deep indigo hues to the palest blues, seen here, hand-dyed batik has nuances of color that are rare in other fabrics. The simple geometric patterns further enhance the Zen-like mood of the room.

cozy sophistication and beauty." —Adam Malka

Smooth and rough finishes are often juxtaposed with one another in this house, and pleasingly tactile upholstery fabrics can be found throughout. Mixing a variety of surface textures in this way brings visual richness, complexity, and tactile abundance to every room. Incorporating handmade and vintage pieces, repurposed fabrics, and furnishings with streamlined modern features adds authenticity and interest to the laid-back, bohemian look and casual atmosphere that we set out to establish.

Though contemporary, architecturally speaking, Adam's home reflects his appreciation for craftsmanship and fondness for artisanal and repurposed elements, seen here in the form of vintage Moroccan rugs, Turkish hemp upholstery, and vintage mid-century modern furniture pieces. It also demonstrates how well tradition and innovation can intersect, resulting in a modern-meets-boho aesthetic with a personalized energy and a welcoming, lived-in quality despite the newness of the building. Everything in this house has been chosen with great care and Adam is very happy living in a home that is tailor-made to suit his preferences.

above Adjacent to the living room, and nestled within a verdant outdoor space, the main terrace allows Adam to make the most of alfresco entertaining. The setting is both functional and atmospheric, the perfect place to enjoy an intimate cocktail hour or a festive party with many guests.

left The open staircase leads to an airy landing where a minimalist backdrop acts as a canvas for a textural macramé wall hanging, a graceful and luxurious plant, a trio of basket-style pendants, and a pair of hemp runners. Windows are kept free of covering to maximize the natural light.

opposite above To give the master bedroom an aura of restful sophistication, we chose to go with an earthy palette of soft browns and creams. We also integrated materials and finishes that keep the room grounded, such as the leather bench, the black-and-cream handmade Indian Bhujodi pillows, and matching throw blanket.

opposite below The pair of armchairs and their pillows are covered in vintage hemp, a fabric similar to linen that is valued for its durability.

In every room of Adam's home, we utilized a neutral backdrop of white, gray, and natural wood as a base to ground a richer palette of warm creams, browns, blues, and blacks. We carefully edited where and how color would flow throughout the house, how every element would fit the overall palette, and the proportions of the hues in each space. When all the elements are layered correctly, even a mix of brown tones can evoke an artistic vibe.

It was also important that cohesion existed inside and out, so the exterior spaces are furnished with equal measures of materials and colors that unite the home to its surroundings while keeping style and nature in focus. The end result is a home that feels current, curated, nurturing, and inviting, and is a reflection of Adam's aesthetic.

As an artist, Adam is very creative on many levels, and he is always on the hunt for vintage and new pieces. I sometimes think he needs another 10 homes to hold all of his ideas! This is the first interior I have worked on for him, but something tells me it won't be the last.

coastal *vibes*

Most of my life has been completely unplanned and determined by luck. In the late 1990s, when I had just opened the Tumbleweed & Dandelion store, I accompanied my boyfriend Jonathan to his cousin Bobby's birthday party. It was there that I met a lovely woman with lots of spunk and even more persuasiveness. I didn't know it at the time, but this chance encounter would end up altering the course of my next 15 years.

Before long, my new acquaintance had convinced me to leave the soirée and drive up to her house so that she could show me a small project for her. She bounced into her brand-new, champagne-colored Mercedes coupe and Jonathan and I climbed into my Jeep CJ-7, which, for those of you who don't know, is a rugged vehicle that is built for speed and clunking, and a far cry from luxurious. We followed her through a pair of massive gates into a five-car garage next to an 11,000-square-foot/1,020-square-meter home. I did my best to play it cool and not let my awe, excitement, and anticipation show through, but I distinctly remember thinking to myself: "Can I do this? Do I actually know anything?"

opposite Outdoor living is one of my favorite aspects of the California lifestyle, and Joni and Jeff Marine's Malibu beach house was designed to take full advantage of that particular opportunity. The main living spaces open up to the stone terrace, where an expandable table means there is always room for one more. Just a few steps from the sandy beach and surf, the blue tiles of the pool capture the ocean's indigo hue.

above The shingled exterior underscores the organic architecture of the building. Reclaimed wooden benches welcome with their simple lines, warm tones, and blue-and-white pillows.

left A view through
the living room to the
ocean beyond is the first
thing visitors see when
they step inside. The
retractable doors invite
light and nature in and
make entertaining easy.
Upholstered pieces and soft
pillows provide irresistible
perches from which to
take in the vistas. The
couple's family and friends
love to gather here to chat
and enjoy a glass of wine.
Set against a backdrop of
enduring wood, the dining
room's ample table, rustic
bench, wicker chairs, and
casual accessories keep
the mood lighthearted
and relaxed.

top left Delicate yet
easy to care for, air
plants are a great option
for low-maintenance
greenery. They are also
good companions for an
assortment of seashells.

middle left Turquoise
accents pop up here and
there to link the home
to its beachside location.
The swirly plates echo the
gentle ripples of the waves.

opposite bottom left The living room has a pale-gray palette that brings to mind the weathered hues of the sun-bleached driftwood on the local beaches. The cottage-style coffee table balances the modernity of the custom-made sofas. Hints of turquoise from the fireplace surround and a collection of urns and pottery add cheerful notes to the muted scheme. The artwork reflects the area's graceful palms and beautiful sunsets.

above The dining room's wooden furniture offers a warm contrast to the white cabinetry of the kitchen and the gray tones of the living room. The built-in storage unit has a mirrored backdrop that not only amplifies the natural light but also draws attention to the shells, glass orbs, and other ocean finds on display, which tie in with the coastal theme of the open-plan space. Clear pendants keep the sea view unobstructed.

opposite The kitchen's tidal blues and surf-washed aqua accents deliver visual snap and anchor the beach house firmly to its coastal location. An azure light pendant overhead complements the pebble-like textured backsplash and the vintage barstools. The island's stone countertop is a one-of-a-kind piece that brings together these bold statement hues with the earthy tones of the printed window shade/blind.

above left The dramatic island top reveals a range of turquoise and greens with infinite tonalities, brown and gold streaks, exotic seams, and tactile textures.

above right The design and color of the backsplash were inspired by the tumbled sea glass that graces the littoral with its polished finish and blue-green hues.

However, it soon became clear that this persuasive ball of energy and I were perfect for one another. Her name is Joni Marine and she has since become a lifelong friend. Over the years, I have been grateful for every challenge with which she and her husband Jeff have presented me. In fact, the Malibu beach house shown on these pages is the sixth home I have decorated for the Marines.

There are views... and then there are Views with a capital V—that sums up one of the most wow-worthy attributes of Joni and Jeff's beach house, its shimmering vistas of the Pacific Ocean. With a footprint of 5,800 square feet/540 square meters, the new-build home was designed by John Kilbane of Archwest Developments and I was part of the process from the ground up, supervising every decision and attending weekly meetings. As homeowners, Joni and Jeff were definitely involved with the project, but they were also very glad to have my input. I remember the building contractor was an ex-marine and I don't think he appreciated me very much at first, but I am proud to say that we became good friends over the course of the project and it showed in our work.

The house sits on a spectacular shoreline and the goal was for the exterior to recall a shingled beach house as opposed to the standard modern white homes that dot the California coastline. The organic architecture looks and feels right for its setting. It is a large house, but it doesn't seem that way because, together with the way we framed the views, the combination of color, furnishings, and accents creates a sense of coziness and intimacy with an emphasis on the beach setting.

The house was designed for ease of movement between indoor and out, so the breezy, bright, and casual interiors offer inviting spaces to share. At ground level, the open-plan kitchen, dining area, and living room spill onto a terrace and a sparkling pool that, in turn, leads to the shore. Reclaimed wood, hints of color, tactile accessories, and a mix of rustic and elegant pieces feel coastal but not too beachy. The end result is a home that fits its idyllic location with a style that speaks of a slower, more relaxed pace of life. This is where casual comfort meets California chic.

above In the spacious master bedroom, a wall of windows opens out onto the balcony, with its glass panels that allow the spectacular Pacific Ocean vista to become part of the decor. Varying shades of blue—from the artwork to the furnishings— enhance the serene coastal theme. Subtle patterns and textures come into play in the rug, curtains, armchairs, and pillows.

opposite above The sea view, the pristine tub, and the shower's glass enclosure bestow a spa-like feel on the bathroom. The fireplace adds to the comfort level and anchors the space, while the blue glass pendant looks as though it has been plucked from the ocean.

opposite below left A seafoam backdrop sets the scene for the guest bedroom's fresh and easy demeanor. The rustic bed, textural layers, and framed shell etchings join together to create a beach cottage setting with a twist on tradition.

opposite below right The reclaimed wooden headboard, an original design by Tumbleweed & Dandelion, adds a textural element.

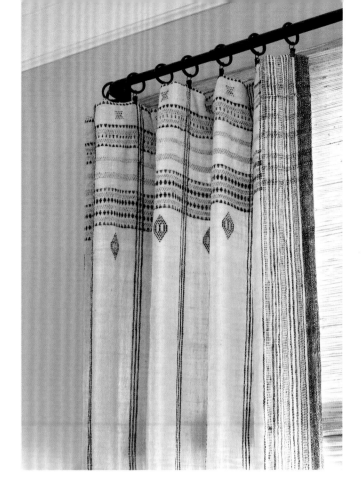

style to *spare*

Any modern architecture enthusiast would jump at the chance to live in a building like this Los Angeles apartment complex. It was designed in the 1930s by Meyer & Holler, the architectural firm that was also responsible for creating Sid Grauman's iconic Chinese and Egyptian Theatres on Hollywood Boulevard, among its many achievements. The complex was reimagined in 2019 as a landmarked enclave, but it has kept its original wood-burning fireplaces, hardwood floors, soaring ceilings, and fine millwork. My clients Laura Pardini and Shawn Ferjanec are two of the lucky residents.

Laura is a professional realtor and she and I met on a staging job. I then also discovered that her husband Shawn is a talented photographer and creative director, whose work has graced the covers of countless fashion magazines, and I have since been buying his art for both my store and my interior-design projects. Beside its pedigree, Laura and Shawn's 1,800-square-foot/167-square-meter apartment has its own unique flavor, which references two of their favorite styles: Old Hollywood glamour and mid-century modern, both of which have remained timeless and avoided anachronism and obscurity.

opposite One of Shawn's fashion photographs picks up on the cheerful coral-and-cream hues of the custom-made embroidered suzani pillow. Curves, angles, and finishes come together and balance one another in the pairing of the geometric side table—a vintage piece from Laura's family—with the soft lines of the modern womb chair. Though from a different era, the mid-century lamp fits well within the inviting setting.

above The curtains' distinctive and original pattern demonstrates the virtues of embracing the artisanal beauty of tribal fabrics while adding a hint of boho flair.

left The living room's effortlessly sophisticated aesthetic emerges from the juxtaposition of Laura and Shawn's two favorite styles, mid-century modern and Old Hollywood, underscored by the muted palette, high ceilings, elegant millwork, and wood floor. Above the vintage fireplace, an early work by graphic designer and collage artist Rex Ray illustrates how well different eras can mix. Wooden tables bring in an organic note, and the fire screen reflects the herringbone pattern of the hearth. Charcoal accents from the pillows, curtains, and rug share a common design thread.

above left In the dining room, gold accents from the chandelier and mirror suggest timeless Hollywood glamour, while the table and Wishbone chairs speak of modern vintage.

above right A custom hand-stenciled design adds depth, visual dimension, and interest to this wall. Even the subtlest detail can bring in a touch of dramatic flair.

opposite Though not big on bold hues, Laura and Shawn fell for the bright color and medallion pattern of the suzani fabric we used to make the kitchen shades/blinds. The decorative textile invigorates the small room and, together with the vintage rug, contributes a well-traveled mood to the space. The white cabinetry tempers these lively colors with the soapstone countertops, dark-hued appliances, and wooden floor bringing definition.

Both eras work well together because they balance each other: mid-century modern is more masculine, featuring straightforward furnishings with slimmed-down profiles, whereas Old Hollywood is more elaborate and dramatic. We kept the latter current by adding in neutral accessories with a touch of modern luxury and kept elements like flooring and walls organic while adding touches of glam.

But what both styles do have in common is that furniture is not intended to be the focal point, so the overall effect relies on touchable fabrics, interesting patterns, and accessories with shiny finishes. Though the mid-century modern look is the prevailing aesthetic of the two, I love how the mix produces an elegant eclecticism.

Homes usually look like their owners and should always reflect their style. Working with Laura and Shawn was a creative and completely wonderful experience. Their taste is consistent, which made it easy to keep the decor flowing from one room to the next.

opposite Positioned above
a woven chair, the rounded
ceramic pieces of a one-
of-a-kind wall hanging by
artist Heather Levine make
an effective and striking
statement. The repeated
circles are in unison with
the shape of the chair,
and their earthy hues are
echoed in the soft pillows.

Both Laura and Shawn lean toward a neutral palette,
so my biggest challenge was to get them to embrace
color. When we painted the dining room, at first we went
with a bold coral shade, but it proved to be too much for
them. My main objective is always to come up with colors,
furniture, and accessories that clients love and with which
they feel comfortable. So we switched to a more subdued
creamy hue but made one wall a standout feature with a
hand-painted stencil design in white and tan, and it sealed
the deal. Overall, staying with soft neutrals like white,
gray, and tan provided the perfect foundation. Layering
monochromatic tones gave us the freedom to add a touch
of quiet drama, such as the living room's vintage window
treatment and statement artwork.

We worked with most of the goods they already had and
consulted on furniture purchasing—among which were the
dining room set and bed—as well as making innovative soft
furnishings out of vintage cloth, including a bold suzani
fabric that they loved and was made into the kitchen's
shades/blinds. It became the star of the space. I love the
kitchen because it makes me feel like I could be anywhere.

The most rewarding part is to see how Laura and Shawn's
home shows their commitment to the building's history,
their appreciation for the eras they love, and how they
honored all with a deeply personal style while staying
true to their shared vision.

above left Calming tones
and soft textures set the
cocoon-like mood of the
sophisticated master
bedroom. The focus is on
textiles, with layers of
linens cozying up the bed,
while the comforter/duvet,
bedskirt, and rug inject
a tactile quality. To add
interest, we hand-stenciled
and painted the wall with
a delicate pattern in a
neutral color.

above right The pillows'
contemporary patterns
relax the formality of the
tufted headboard.

heart and *soul*

For some, getting away from the rigors of work means grabbing a sleeping bag and going completely off the grid. For me, it's the call of a gentler kind of wild that pulls me to my cottage way up north in New York State.

This is not an area that I discovered by chance. I grew up in the little town of Dunkirk on Lake Erie. My father was an architect who worked for I.M. Pei as well as Richard Meier. My mother was (and is) beautiful in every way. For all the courage and gumption my father gave my siblings and me, my mother matched it with grace and kindness. We were a perfectly imperfect crew.

When I was in the fifth grade, our favorite neighbors took my parents to see a lake house where they summered, which was up for sale. It was only 10 miles from our home and way out of my parents' price range. The sellers, however, took a shine to my mom and dad and agreed to carry the mortgage to help them finance the purchase. Suddenly we really lived on the lake. We spent every day at the beach, body surfing and making bonfires. The story of my life truly began here and it has never gotten old.

opposite Adirondack chairs are a traditional feature in cottages like ours and a meaningful complement to the rusticity of the deck, which is a favorite spot to observe nature and watch sailboats on the lake in spring and summer. When fall comes, we can still enjoy the views and the autumnal colors but in the comfort of warm jackets instead of shorts and T-shirts.

above I enjoy making painted signs out of old boards—I like to think of it as "driftwood therapy."

above On one of my cross-country trips to take furniture from the West Coast to a job in New York, I realized that I needed a new sofa for the cottage, so I loaded this one, a Tumbleweed classic, on the truck. It's comfortable, accommodating, and (thanks to the slipcover) easy to maintain. My father rescued the kids' table and several little chairs from an old school. They hold much sentimental value.

opoosite White walls, plenty of windows, and blue-and-white patterned textiles make the room feel cool and crisp. On a clear day you can see all the way across the lake to Canada.

Fast forward to 2007, when my good friend Karen took me to see a cottage on the lake of my childhood. I was enchanted but not sure, and I remember the owner, a local school teacher, said: "I think you will regret it if you pass this by." I know now that she was right. Together with my sister Colleen and her husband Danny, Jonathan and I took the plunge and bought the little ramshackle house in Van Buren Point, a historic town that dates back to 1784 and was once the home of Mark Twain. This is a unique community where houses are passed down for generations. Some of the cottages here have belonged to the same families for more than 80 years.

For Jonathan and me, the cottage is a true sanctuary —regenerative, fun, and always different. We don't bring any work drama here. It is a place where we can recharge and regroup, but also remember, because this cottage is laden with the lasting legacy of cherished memories and authentic charm. It's healing to the soul.

opposite For fun, we
painted the partial wall
that conceals the stairs
to the bedrooms using
chalkboard paint. It is
now an interactive focal
point, where all who come
to visit leave us messages.
My brother Sean gifted me
the plant stand, which also
makes a great Champagne
bucket when needed.

If an owner in Van Buren Point does eventually choose
to sell, they often leave the furniture for the next owner.
Many items in our cottage—the porch sofa and wicker
chairs, the dining-room table, chairs, and credenza/
sideboard, and more—are pieces that I kept and painted to
give them a new lease of life. Not wanting to alter the spirit
of the place, and hoping to keep down the costs, I went
with found vintage and flea-market pieces. One summer,
when my uncle Mike came to town, we hit the local yard
and garage sales and got lots of "cheap and cheerful"
items. If I see it and I like it, I buy it, and then revive those
items in need of a facelift: no furniture can hide from my
paintbrush, except, maybe, pre-loved family heirlooms.

The interiors keep evolving to this day, but right from the
beginning, the decoration was purely functional. I didn't
want it to feel overly "done," so the cottage is only lightly
curated—sea glass and good bedding take the stage here.

above The fireplace, built
with local stones, is original
to the house. Next year
we are planning to lift the
cottage because it's leaning
to one side and needs to be
leveled. We will then redo
the floor with wood planks
but, for now, the carpet will
do. The sisal rug softens its
color and material and
adds natural texture.

previous pages There is an easy flow from the living room to the dining area and the kitchen beyond. All the rooms share a similar decor because they each are mostly furnished with cast-offs from one provenance or another. The dining-room furniture consists of leftover treasures from the previous owner. I painted the chairs and the credenza/sideboard, but I go back and forth regarding the fate of the table, which remains untouched for now.

left Floral centerpieces from Wild Blossom Hollow (www.wildblossomhollow. com) take their cues from the seasons. The flowering apple-blossom branches hold special significance because they came from a tree that my father planted many years ago.

opposite The credenza/ sideboard is ideal for storing table linen, silverware, and dishes, while the surface is handy for buffet-style serving. An original map of Van Buren Point and a plan of the cottage on the wall highlight its unique history.

My world is busy and being here anchors my soul. If I could make a living gluing seashells to mirrors, I would never leave.

opposite The narrow galley kitchen retains its bygone charm and appears more spacious thanks to its white-painted walls. Removing the doors from the upper cupboards allows convenient access to the dishes. In a small house, storage and functionality go hand in hand.

right Small appliances save valuable floor space. Tucked under the stairs, the vintage table adds workspace and a place to store baskets filled with cookware essentials.

above Rustic crunchy bread, wrapped in vintage French linen cloths, is always on hand to smear with butter and jam or for making fresh sandwiches. Life at the cottage is always easy, and hearty meals are a big part of our daily rituals.

I just wanted to enjoy the environment and not focus on creating a show home, so I took a go-with-the-flow approach. Sticking to that goal actually made it easy to create the laid-back style I was looking for. The great thing is that it has come together organically because it takes in the vintage patinas and handmade details of artisanal goods and inherited pieces that reflect the time and place.

The cottage isn't especially large, but with a good-sized living room and dining room, an enclosed porch, four bedrooms, a bathroom, and a small kitchen, we have more than enough space. The beauty of the rooms is that they seem to wrap around you like a warm embrace, making you feel secure and right at home. Each space is meant to generate a sense of belonging and genuine reassurance that you are welcome to come as you are.

right Nicknamed Moby
Dick, the enormous fish was
caught by my dad and was
the biggest one I have ever
seen come out of the lake.
The nightstands are new,
but they work—perhaps it's
because, with the Turkish
towels used as curtains and
the simplicity of the bed,
the room has a youthful,
summer-camp feel.

opposite below left
We are always ready to pack a bag, grab some towels, and hit the beach, especially during the warmer months.

opposite below right
We have a wonderful large family, but not a lot of heirlooms. These sports trophies were won by my uncle Brainard Parson.

left Our new bedding is ever so soft and cozy—and it is eco friendly, too.

below This bedroom has a French vibe and is very romantic. It has lovely pale blue accents, including my mother's first dresser/chest of drawers, which I painted. Other details include a sweet lamp, a rustic bench, and a black-and-white photograph of a young Brigitte Bardot.

For me, it's important to stay connected
to pieces from the past, and be surrounded
with lovely memories that stir my emotions
and make my heart full.

opposite I adore (and couldn't resist) this Tom Everhart print of Charlie Brown and Snoopy.

above I love how the slanted ceiling, the beadboard, and the sound of the floorboards underfoot give this bedroom so much charm. The vintage wicker dresser/chest of drawers, which came from my aunt Dottie's cottage, and its antique wooden counterpart add character as well as practical storage. The nubby bouclé chair offers an invitation to cozy up and sit a while.

The building is well insulated and has a large fireplace (essential during the brutal New York winters), so we can use it year round, work permitting. We have been here when the summer days seem endless and we can go swimming and kayaking and celebrate the 4th of July with family and friends, and in the winter when the snow cloaks everything in white and silence and we can bask in the radiant glow of the fire. But whatever the season, there's an open invitation to all.

The bedrooms upstairs share a commonality of weightless colors, and are simply furnished but in a way that's cozy and restful, and with thoughtfully placed pieces to allow for lots of breathing room that show how you can live large even in a small space.

I so love this little house with all its imperfections, such as the uneven floors and all the quirky angles. My world is busy and being here anchors my soul. If I could make a living gluing seashells to mirrors, I would never leave. I haven't made any big changes, but I do small jobs here and there and someday, maybe, there will be a new kitchen. Time will tell. We recently got a new tin roof and we are constantly painting and upgrading, but the cottage is still a ramshackle treasure, just as it was when we found it. No doubt it will be a work in progress for quite a while, but that's part of the fun, as long as we keep its history ever present. For me, it's important to stay connected to pieces from the past, and be surrounded by lovely memories that stir my emotions and make my heart full.

above The lake-facing front porch remains the same as it was on the original cottage. The sofa came with the house. I toyed with the idea of replacing it with a new one but, truth be told, my father spent one night on this sofa before he passed away, so I couldn't bear to part with it. We summered in Van Buren Point as children and I know the joy it gave my dad to think of all of us here.

opposite The life preserver used to be on our 17-foot/5-metre-long sailboat, but it was lost a long time ago. Years later, I found it again— in the garage of a house that my cousin had bought, which had previously belonged to a sailor. Talk about serendipity!

mediterranean *moments*

A while back, I became involved with the construction of Jeff and Jeannine Bird's home in Anaheim, California. Then Covid-19 hit, but luckily we were able to work through it. Their home is a 90-minute drive from my office, so the reduced traffic during the pandemic was a blessing. This was a very special project for me because it's a circular home, which is so unusual. I worked closely with the architect Semion Tafipolsky and he really elevated our plans for the site.

Jeff and Jeannine have traveled extensively in Europe and were enchanted by the beauty of Italian villages and Mediterranean architecture. They loved the richness, accessibility, colors, and time-honored materials that speak of history and give these old houses their soul. So it makes perfect sense that, when they set out to build their dream home, they were inspired by the simple beauty of the Mediterranean lifestyle.

The couple envisioned a Spanish Revival design, and it gave me a simple idea: to rotate the original plan so that the rooms would surround a courtyard living space, which would allow Jeff and Jeannine to make the most of the balmy California weather.

opposite The high-ceilinged living room demanded lighting that would make a statement, such as this grouping of spheres. The effect is magnified by their reflections in the curved mirror, which we designed specifically for the space along with the stone fireplace, bookcases, and curved sofas. The latter are a flexible option, as they can also be put next to each other to face the hearth.

above A side table made from a tree stump is texturally beautiful.

opposite The bookcases
are designed to follow
the curve of the wall. We
treated the poplar wood to a
weathered finish with layers
of non-toxic paint, which
were applied by hand and
rubbed to give it an aged
appearance. The textural
objects displayed on the
shelves add to the ambience.
In the center of the room,
the soft bouclé fabric of the
circular ottoman softens
the rugged stonework of the
bespoke fireplace.

below The dining room's
tall, arched windows have
more than an architectural
impact. They draw the eye
upward and have a light-
enhancing quality that
brings out the honey tone
of the handsome table and
cane-backed dining chairs.
With their wing-like curved
shape, the chairs are a
current take on a traditional
style. The chandelier
overhead adds a geometric
element and a touch of
contemporary style.

The end goal was to celebrate age-old beauty, but with the added comfort of a modern cocoon. Semion created exactly what I had in mind—we added a courtyard entrance and built the home to fit the land. When you open the doors and feel the breeze, it's like being at a resort.

The construction alone took just under three years from start to finish. This was by far the most difficult journey I have been on. Circumstances were not on our side—building a 6,000-square-foot/557-square-meter home during the pandemic meant we had to contend with a shortage of materials as well as unavailable subcontractors, which caused many delays. Somehow we overcame all these challenges, though it took the expression "a labor of love" to a whole new level.

We didn't want to create something that looked brand new, so for a timeless effect we used reclaimed materials and real stone, and prioritized fine craftsmanship. That said, it was also important that the interiors feel fresh and current. Though they gave me a lot of creative freedom, Jeff and Jeannine were very involved and we collaborated on the many ideas—in fact, by the end of the project, I believe Jeff had become entirely capable of building a home on his own.

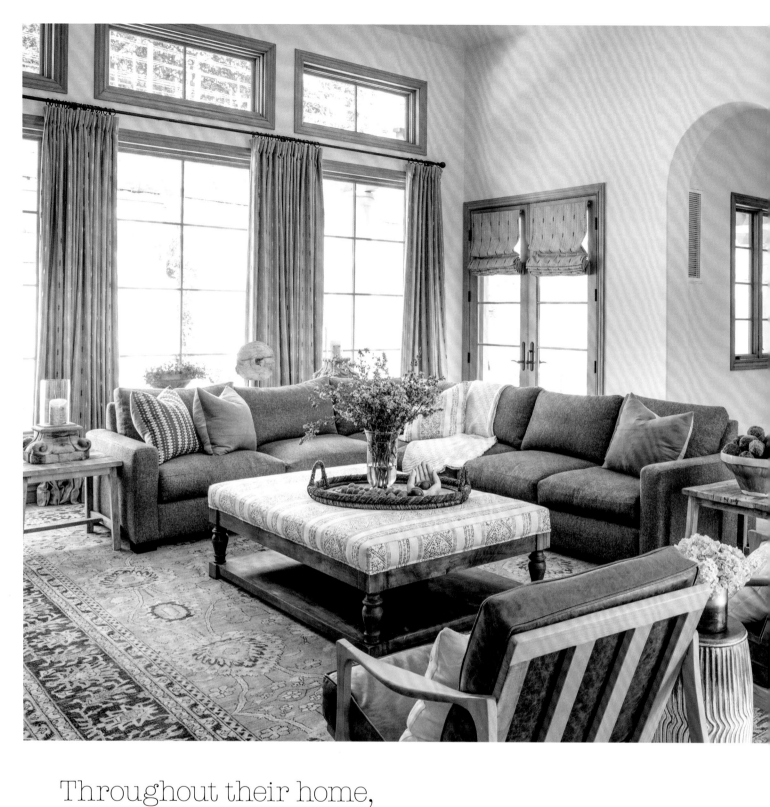

Throughout their home,
Jeff and Jeannine chose the most beautiful
rugs and fabrics that bestow
a subtle opulence and grace.

opposite The family room is where the couple, their children, and their pets share most of their time together, so it needed to be casual but with stylish comfort. We custom-built the ottoman—to which a slipcover can be added to keep the delicate Indian block-printed fabric safe from sticky fingers when necessary—and went with sofas upholstered in a worry-free performance material.

below The wall-mounted panels and the rustic credenza/sideboard accessorized with a textural basket, gilded candelabras, and shapely ceramics reference Italian furnishings of yore. Their earthy tones harmonize with the chair and the side table. Throughout the house, with the exception of the master bathroom, we used tiles that mimic hardwood for the floors so that they would withstand wear and tear.

right Though small, accessories with the right texture and color play a big part in keeping the room on theme.

far right A light gray wash gives the bleached Douglas fir of the bookcase its aged appearance.

left Texture, subtle colors,
discreet patterns, and
European-style details like
the vanity, mirror, marble
backsplash, and tiles are
the heavy lifters that bring
light touches of old-world
charm to the powder room.
The cabinet is finished with
hand-rubbed paint.

opposite We lit the
succession of graceful
arches in this hallway with
three identical clear-glass
lanterns to emphasize the
architectural features.
Vintage runners share
the limelight with the
15-foot/4.5-meter-tall
mahogany doors. The
simple, minimal console
table unites modern lines
with rustic wood, while the
windowpane mirror lends
a light and airy feel to the
narrow space.

To meet the couple's 21st-century requirements but still
imbue the rooms with a sense of belonging to another time
and place, we hand-built many pieces to fit the spaces and
applied a patinated finish to the living-room bookcases.
We balanced those old-world elements with comfortable
yet stylish furnishings in order to give each room its own
personality. For instance, the living room unites rustic
pieces with on-trend curved sofas—I love their versatility—
and is all about softness and low-key elegance. In the
family room, we layered rustic wood and vintage artifacts
with furniture that leans toward contemporary forms. And
in the kitchen, stone, tiles, and rough wooden surfaces
express the Mediterranean vernacular with gusto.

above left and right Just
off the hallway is a small
bathroom, in which the
marble backsplash and
stone basin look as though
they have been taken from
an Italian farmhouse.
Though the marble is new,
the sink was formerly used
by painters in our studio
—a perfect example of
imaginative recycling.

above We chose these tiles for the kitchen
wall because they are the epitome of vintage
Mediterranean style inspired by sun-drenched
courtyards. Although they are new, their blue-and-
white pattern includes imitation scuffs and spots
that provide a sense of age-old authenticity.

opposite With stones, rough timber, aged wood,
and tiles that conceal the hood and create the feel
of an Italian farmhouse, the alcove that houses
the range is the kitchen's focal point. We topped
the custom island with blue stone, which
complements the tiles and adds character.

We balanced the old-world elements with comfortable yet stylish furnishings in order to give each room its own personality.

above Jeannine wanted one room of the house to have a sense of glamour, and it made the most sense to dress up the spacious master bedroom. We chose a custom bed with lilac-hued velvet upholstery to match the tufted wall behind, which serves as an oversized headboard. To amp up the glamour even further, we added a selection of silvery pillows.

above The bathroom is an ode to femininity. The ethereal mother-of-pearl chandelier flirts with the contemporary tub to foster a mood that is both modern and romantic. The all-white scheme gets a little boost of color from the faded blue and soft aqua of the shades/blinds, while the gleaming white wall tiles add to the peaceful, serene atmosphere of the space.

On the opposite end of the design spectrum, Jeff and Jeannine's master suite is a tribute to the glamorous attributes of the famed *dolce vita*, with a more feminine palette and vintage glass mirrors. It reflects the care and attention to detail that they displayed during the design process. Throughout their home, they chose the most beautiful rugs and fabrics that bestow a subtle opulence and grace. I believe that residential design should be curated and that you must take time to look for the right pieces rather than trying to fill the space quickly.

Both Jeff and Jeannine have relatives who live in the neighborhood, so they wanted a home they could enjoy as a family and where they could entertain their loved ones. And they got it. When it was all said and done, we had achieved exactly what we aimed for: luxurious and rustic interiors whose timeless beauty belies the newness of the home.

This house is very dear to me—it was challenging to complete, but the results are worth it and I fell in love with the whole Bird family along the way. We got through a pandemic together and we created a home they really love. For me, the most wonderful part was seeing their joy as we got to the finish line.

pacific *paradise*

When you are looking for your dream home, location is everything. So it's no wonder that, with its fabled beaches and its reputation as the home of celebrities and leading entertainment-industry figures, Malibu holds an almost mythical status.

But for David Corvo and his wife Michele Willens, their beachfront home in the star-studded, exclusive Malibu Colony really is a dream come true, and not just because of its location. David and Michele are primarily based in New York City, where David is the senior executive producer at NBC (overseeing shows such as *Dateline: The Last Day*) and Michele is a journalist, author, and playwright. When time permits, their Malibu home is a welcome escape and a place where they can kick back away from the demands and pressures of their professions.

We met through mutual friends. I have always loved David and Michele—they are kind, patient, reasonable, and very funny—and working with them was a creative pleasure.

opposite This staircase leads to the upper floor, where a balcony overlooks the living room and the Pacific Ocean beyond. Ingenuity meets practicality with built-in niches under the stairs that offer space for favorite items and personal mementoes from movie posters to awards. The translucent quality of the chandelier evokes the surface of tumbled seaglass.

above Incorporating coastal items, such as driftwood and glass beads, makes for an authentic presence.

overleaf A selective use of furnishings with vibrant pops of color and modern silhouettes, together with one-of-a-kind contemporary artwork, ties the living room together effectively. The mellow tones of the rug and ottomans balance the brighter and deeper hues of the sofa and armchairs. A variety of patterns and textures adds diversity to the mix and creates visual harmony. Floor-to-ceiling glass doors facilitate the flow of natural light into the space.

"Lizzie doesn't have a preconceived notion of how a home should look. She responds to each unique space and uses her talent to bring out the best in it." —David Corvo

left The dining room is open to the kitchen and the living room, accentuating the home's informal and relaxed design and enabling a seamless flow from one space to the next. For the dining room, we opted for a sturdy and textural vintage farmhouse table that can accommodate dinner parties, and chairs that can be moved outdoors when taking festivities to the deck. Ordinary recessed lighting and sconces that fade into the background are eschewed in favor of a centerpiece pendant light with some serious pizzazz.

above The fully equipped kitchen stands by for entertaining. The backsplash and the base of the island pick up some of the many blue tones of the ocean.

above David, a senior executive producer at NBC, is the recipient of countless News & Documentary Emmy Awards, so many in fact that several of his trophies are kept in a basket rather than being on display throughout the house.

above right Though the home is primarily a place to enjoy work-free days, a custom desk offers just the right spot for Michele and David to jot down their ideas for new books and shows when creativity strikes.

The house formerly belonged to Michele's father and had undergone some modifications eight years ago. Over the course of six months, we reimagined and updated the living room, sunroom, office, all the bedrooms, the theater, and the upper deck. Most recently, we have been working on the main deck as well, and I am still just as enthusiastic about this project as I was at the beginning.

Spanning two stories above the Pacific Ocean, the interiors are spacious and airy with the living room and sunroom opening out to the panoramic views, and with plenty of space for entertaining and relaxing. The sunroom, which butts right up to the ocean deck, is a recent addition. It is David's favorite space, for which he is quick to credit me for "not trying to out-decorate Mother Nature and instead designing a room that lets the beauty in." There is no better place to read a book, nap, or have family and friends over, which is something Michele and David love to do when they are here. They are gracious hosts and often bring together interesting groups of people to share time and food.

above The sunroom exemplifies how a space can integrate with its environment yet not upstage it. Here, it comes down to a palette that alludes to the seascape and a setting that honors the location. Carefree materials, such as the vegan leather of the sofa and the outdoor fabric of the benches and pillows, invite unhurried moments and embrace the uplifting power of a restorative environment.

opposite With its woven wicker and bamboo frame, this table has a hint of the tropics and a texture that balances the smooth poplar wood of the built-in seating. Its curvy shape also softens the angular lines of the window seat, bench, and windows.

David and Michele love Italy and the ocean, and their decor and design choices reflect their fondness for both—think Capri meets colorful beach house.

It was important to give the sunroom the comfortably stylish yet coastal atmosphere it called for, at the same time as keeping it void of nautical clichés. Setting the tone with a cool palette of whites and blues felt like the natural choice and gives the space an ethereal quality, while wood and leather add warmth and ensure the room is grounded.

To facilitate conversation and daydreams, we custom-built the large, stalwart leather sectional, which can take a lot of traffic and is basically people-proof, and the window banquette and corner bench. The ample seating makes it easy for the couple and their guests to take full advantage of the view and enjoy a front-row seat to watch the tide roll in and witness Malibu's unforgettable sunsets. The shelves had to be configured to allow space for the bench and kept low to display artwork and watch television.

For the other spaces, we went with a soft palette that recalls the white caps of the nearby waves and brought in a contemporary look with furnishings upholstered with materials that will take a lot of wear and tear. Though Italian style may bring to mind deep wine shades and rich earth tones, the use of a neutral backdrop here lends a sense of airy freshness. To keep everything looking and feeling lively and relaxed, we also included pieces infused with energetic colors that speak of modernity. Used with restraint, these bolder hues create focal points.

Though each room has its own distinct personality and function, they all share a touch of blue that brings to mind the opaque depths of the Pacific and the infinite hues of the sky—whether sapphire, indigo, or other variations on the theme, either on statement pieces, such as the living-room sofa and the kitchen backsplash, or on smaller items via pillows, throws, and rugs. Even the theater's overall mostly muted palette boasts a brilliant blue feature wall.

As I mentioned earlier, for David and Michele, this home is highly prized for much more than its location. It represents Michele's father's legacy, now imprinted with the couple's own style, and is a special place where they can gather with their family and friends, share meaningful times together, and make new memories.

above We named this room the "theater"—as in movie theater—because it's where the family gathers to watch the news, TV shows, and of course movies, while enjoying drinks and food thanks to the built-in cabinets where treats are kept on hand. Posters nod to Hollywood and add to the entertainment-driven atmosphere of the space.

right We wanted to elevate the room from its former decor to a more modern look. With that goal in mind, we constructed a wooden wall and brought in furnishings with a youthful, retro vibe, including a custom sofa upholstered in chevron-print fabric and soft furnishings with touches of coral.

Spanning two stories above the Pacific Ocean, the interiors are spacious and airy with panoramic views and plenty of space for entertaining and relaxing.

overleaf Since the house is very modern, it seemed appropriate to keep the bedrooms cozy as a reminder of the cottage that once stood here. We leaned into a simple aesthetic that is a bit more old school but has subtly contemporary undertones. Though the furnishings are simple, the linens, chair, art, and accessories gently bring the room into the present day.

home *couture*

A home for sale that Tumbleweed & Dandelion staged in Encino, California brought us together with Beka and Ben Tischker. I say "us" because this project is a perfect example of teamwork involving myself, one of my designers, Mkayel Bojakijian, and several other people associated with Tumbleweed & Dandelion.

Beka and Ben are a dynamic young couple with eclectic tastes and a penchant for interiors that celebrate creative, innovative ideas. They welcome contemporary visions with a sense of glamour and a playfully daring spirit—rock star meets Southern belle. They are both in the music industry and run their own company, so the house is in constant motion with not only meetings and parties but also with their children and pets. Their energy and creativity are infectious.

I call their style "haute home," as it reminds me of the distinguishing qualities of haute couture: It is luxurious and one-of-a-kind, with an emphasis on craftsmanship. Their new 4,600-square-foot/425-square-meter Encino home, complete with a pool and tennis court in a beautiful setting, offers the ideal solutions tailor-made for their busy lives and love of entertaining.

opposite Juxtaposing items, colors, shapes, and artworks that are visually stimulating gives this corner its edgy, modern-glam mood. The emerald-green curvy sofa is made even brighter by shimmering gold pillows, elongated black sconces and circular tables, and a poster that alludes to owner Ben Tischker's French roots.

above In spite of their eras, a vintage French loveseat upholstered in a tapestry-like fabric—a work of art in itself—and a 1935 American oil painting are perfectly at home in the contemporary dining room and speak to Ben and his wife Beka's eclectic taste and appreciation of finer things.

overleaf The rug's artful bold motifs pull together the dining-room palette into a strong, tactile statement. A graphic 1940s chandelier hangs above the shapely table with its chairs dressed in white cowhide. Gold accents from the table base and chairs highlight their chic and smart design.

opposite In the living room, glass, metal, and wood are unified by their sleek forms and finishes, and by a cream-and-black palette. The color combination continues with the black shelves and displayed accessories.

right There is an art to mixing periods. With its union of the modern sofa and classic loveseat with the contemporary table and chairs (shown on previous pages) and a vintage mid-century buffet (featured here), the dining room successfully blends the eclectic mix that embodies Beka and Ben's style.

below The shelving unit is the feature element of the living room and designed to offer the freedom to rearrange the objects on display. The sofas and chairs are layered in soft fabrics that add warmth to the room while offsetting the cooler aspects stemming from the lines and materials of the coffee table.

overleaf The wallpaper brings graphic impact to the wall that frames the entrance to the foyer from the living room. The design of the credenza/sideboard complements the dramatic effect.

The design concept was to create spaces that would reflect their preference for modern bespoke furniture and accessories with sumptuous touches, plush accents, and refined materials for an unabashedly glamorous interior. To achieve our goal, we turned to palettes ranging from warm neutrals in the living room and bedroom to the jewel tones of the dining room and office.

The living room has a rich yet restrained palette that works in contrasting pairs, in both color and texture. A warm creamy color is the foundational hue that we lavished on the sofas, chairs, and curtains, while an ebony

shelving unit grounds the space. The combination works to highlight the room's contemporary feel, but Beka and Ben don't shy away from strong color elsewhere in the house.

Case in point: the dining room, in which vibrant hues are pulled together with the multi-toned splashes of the rug. And let's not forget the office with its crimson velvet wall—inspired by an interior that Ben had seen in Paris—and golden chairs. I am proud to say I introduced Mkayel to the red velvet. In return, he brought Beka, Ben, and me endless joy with his design choices, including the dining room's green velvet sofa, which I would love for my own home.

above left The foyer heralds Beka and Ben's connection to the music world with a vintage mid-century record cabinet and a wallpaper mural honoring the Alabama building that housed the famed Muscle Shoals Sound Studio.

above right The wet bar was revamped by Mkayel and comes in handy for entertaining, and as a place for mixing cocktails. The gently aged cabinets, mirror, and bar stool are a fitting match for the gold bars and vintage hardware.

right The bedroom
is a realm of calm with a
soft neutral palette and
a sophisticated composition
of cozy elements. The
accent wall sports a discreet
geometric wallpaper that
adds dimension to the room.

above The pampering
bathroom feels luxe, serene,
and lovely with an inviting
tub that commands center
stage and an artful mural
that brings nature within
reach in the form of an
exotic design. The tropical
plants signal the laid-back
ambience of an island
getaway. Floating shelves
are subtly chic, the rug adds
a vintage feel, and the coral
chair strikes a vibrant note.

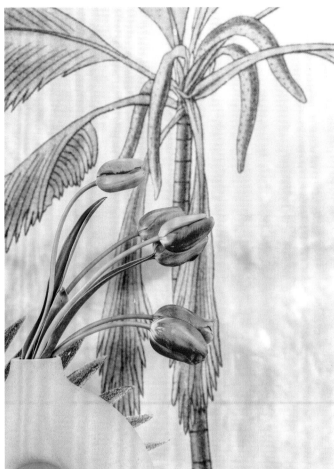

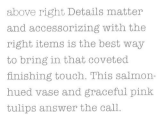

above right Details matter
and accessorizing with the
right items is the best way
to bring in that coveted
finishing touch. This salmon-
hued vase and graceful pink
tulips answer the call.

Mkayel is responsible for elevating the master bedroom, as well as the bathroom, the family room, the living room, and the bar, which was an existing built-in. I suggested painting it black and adding mirrors and gold bars, then Mkayel took it to another level with gorgeous vintage hardware and styling.

We all worked together on the entry—the Muscle Shoals wallpaper idea was Ben's and we just executed it. The photo of the legendary Alabama music studio holds a special meaning for Beka and Ben, symbolizing their connection to the music world. It is also a sentimental reminder of a place that was once a recording mecca for rhythm and blues, rock, and pop artists in the 1960s and 1970s.

Beka and Ben formed a deep bond with Mkayel during the design process—it could even be said that once Mkayel fell under Beka's spell, I became the proverbial third wheel in the relationship. It was clear that Mkayel had a great deal of passion for this project. Beka and Ben wanted to be surprised and he delivered in spades—even going as far as to "borrow" some of my French posters for them.

This whole project is the result of a priceless collaboration between Mkayel, Beka and Ben, and myself. My team and I were very lucky to meet this creative couple when we did and we have enjoyed such a productive partnership with them ever since. I firmly believe that every home should have its own point of view and this one certainly does. It exudes vibrancy, diversity, and personality, and is a mirror image of its owners. It is the happy place for their delightful, happy selves. And the beat goes on!

above We were going for a cool wood wall when Ben mentioned the decor in a *hôtel particulier* (grand townhouse) that he had visited in Paris and the die was cast. The seductive red velvet tufted wall went up, transforming a plain wall into a stunning accent. The wow factor was instant. The ornate antique marquetry desk has been in Ben's family for years. The modern gold velvet chairs make a beautiful and brilliant counterpoint.

opposite Luxurious leather-bound tomes evoke those found in an old French *bibliotheque*.

"I love how the mix of old French pieces
with the modern twist of the chairs
and the sexy velvet wall
makes such a statement." –Beka Tischker

above it *all*

My friend and client Vicki Gordon introduced me to her friend Lesli Linka Glatter, who, at the time, was looking for someone to decorate her Manhattan apartment. Lesli had already met with some other designers, but in the end I won the commission and it was a real pleasure to work with her. Lesli is dynamic and brave, and a force to be reckoned with. She is a director of films and network, cable, and premium television dramas including projects for Netflix, Apple TV, and Showtime, among others. Her directorial accomplishments and awards are endless—think *Homeland*, *The Newsroom*, *The Morning Show*, and so many more. She is also the current president of the Directors Guild of America. Yet, in spite of her high-octane work life, Lesli is kind and inspiring, and a tireless mentor to others.

Though most of her work is in Los Angeles, she also needed a *pied-à-terre* in New York City. She found what she was looking for in a loft located in a 1906 building that once was a factory, then a department store, before it was reinvented as an apartment complex in one of the city's most historically rich neighborhoods. The loft was in good shape but in need of updating. This is where I came into the picture.

opposite Talent runs in the family. A pair of black-and-white photographs by Lesli's cousin Lawrence Beck is given place of pride over the sofa. The inviting and comfortable low-profile furniture is perfectly suited to the room. Pillows provide color without overwhelming the space.

above The built-in shelves, now painted black, offer a stage for art books, modern and rustic items, and photographs that speak to Lesli's many interests and treasured memories.

overleaf The living room exemplifies how mid-century elements come together to create a nod to the past, while streamlined sofas embrace the present. The bookshelves draw the eye upward and emphasize the ceiling height. A neutral-toned rug plays dual roles in grounding the furnishings and defining this area of the open-plan living space.

One of Lesli's best-known projects was the acclaimed television series *Mad Men*, which was widely praised for its stylish visual flair and helped to bring mid-century design back into the mainstream. So it seemed appropriate for me to channel the era's iconic style but with a twist: a gentle dose of "cool NYC artist."

When you step into Lesli's home, you are surrounded by authentic mid-century pieces set within the timeless chic of a serene and muted palette. This is an interior that marries substance with style. With its 14-foot/4.3-meter-high ceiling and walnut floor with an ebony glaze, the open-plan living space was the anchor and the starting point for the design. However, due to the building being a co-op, we couldn't make structural alterations—the ductwork and columns had to remain in place, so we had to incorporate them and make it work.

Lesli wanted to be able to circulate freely around the furniture, so the next challenge was to divide up the all-in-one hallway, living room, and dining room without resorting to physical barriers. Using the furniture to define each zone did the trick. For instance, we arranged the sofas to create a room within the open floor plan and positioned one of them in a way that alludes to a separate hallway.

above left Though from different times and places, the art deco chair (one of a pair) and the Moroccan pouf are united by their colors and curvaceous lines. The tall, slender side table offers room for displaying favorite ceramics without competing with the items showcased on the shelves.

above One of the two sofas provides a visual separation between the living room and hallway, where a pair of vintage lamps on an original credenza/ sideboard frames a painting by Lesli's aunt Rosemarie Beck. Characterized by its free-form walnut base and glass top, a vintage coffee table designed by Adrian Pearsall sits atop a rug featuring an ombré effect that contributes to the room's aura of quiet sophistication.

above left The dining-room chandelier, with its contrasting finishes, makes for a fresh take on mid-century form. Its wide-reaching size is perfect for grand spaces.

above right Curtains fashioned from Bhujodi fabric dress up the dining-room windows while imparting a subtly cosmopolitan vibe.

Throughout the home, the aesthetic is achieved by remaining steadfast to the clean lines, low profile, and quiet elegance of the mid-century style that Lesli favors. With the exception of two chairs and some artworks belonging to Lesli, and the existing built-in shelving on the back wall (which we reconfigured and painted black), we furnished the 2,000-square-foot/185-square-meter loft with authentic vintage pieces and included different textures and finishes to add warmth. We accessorized minimally in order to personalize the rooms but not clutter them.

Although she was highly instrumental in the selection of furniture, fabrics, and accessories, Lesli didn't see the loft until it was completely done. When the big reveal took place, her reaction said it all: "I thought Lizzie got my aesthetic, but, I have to admit, when I stood outside my loft door, about to enter for the first time, I panicked! What if I hated it? What if it wasn't me? But the minute I walked in, I was home. To say I was thrilled beyond belief is simply an understatement. Lizzie channeled me completely."

opposite The living space opens into the dining room, so the colors and materials had to be in sync yet still allow each room its own identity. The warm honey tones of the acacia-wood chairs with light and airy cane seats and backs, the refurbished mid-century table, and the credenza/sideboard give the dining room its golden glow.

opposite The clean lines of the cutting-edge kitchen offer a functional and beautifully organized space. The smooth quartz countertop, sleek white Italian cabinetry, and gleaming appliances balance the richness of the ebony-glazed walnut flooring, which is further softened by the texture of a woven jute rug in a blend of warm, earthy colors.

above right Glass and stone wall tiles in white and gray partner to create a simple, crisp, and elegant backsplash.

Lesli also said of her new home: "I love the sense of space, and I feel a peace in NYC that I've never experienced." Her words are the ultimate compliment and I thought, as they say in the movie business, "That's a wrap!"

Witnessing your clients' happiness and delight when their home is completed is one of the most rewarding aspects of my work. Sometimes, discovering what resonates with a client can be tricky, but in Lesli's case it was very clear to me. Her affinity for her craft, her own artistic sense of style, and her endearing personality made this project so much more than a job. It has been fun, easy, and above all fulfilling. Here, the *Mad Men* vibe is undeniably present: understated but quietly glamorous, capturing a mood of nostalgia for a time when life might not have necessarily been better, but it certainly looked good.

above Family and friends from near and far are greeted by the worldly decor of the guest bedroom. The custom alder-wood queen bed is dressed with linens in neutral tones and accessorized with a monochrome throw and colorful pillows from around the world. The buffalo photograph over the bed speaks to open spaces and adventurous travels.

above right The bathroom was updated with alderwood panels for the tub and vanity. The large mirror creates the illusion of a larger space.

right A mid-century credenza/sideboard and chair cozy up the guest room, while a photograph of a longhorn keeps a watchful eye over the scene.

left Lesli's own bedroom is a study in calm. Furnishings and patterns are kept to a minimum to make this a restful private realm. The gray palette gets subtle hints of color via the coverlet, pillow, and Moroccan rug. Texture comes into play with the upholstery of the custom bed, the inviting bouclé material of the chair, and the plushness of the rug.

modern *alchemy*

When I look at the homes and the people featured in this book, I see a common thread. By that I mean a lot of my work has come as a result of referrals from former clients who have become lifelong friends and introduced me to their family members, business associates, friends, and acquaintances. That in itself is as big a compliment as one can get as a designer and I am very appreciative of the confidence they have bestowed on me. How this project came about is a perfect example.

There is something to be said for chance encounters. Little did I know when I met Molly and Blake Macleod at a wedding that this happy occasion would lead to an even happier one, at least for me! In this instance, Molly's brother Stephen is married to Isabelle Davis and Isabelle is Vicki Gordon's daughter. Both Vicki and Isabelle's homes are featured in this book, as well as that of Vicki's friend Lesli Glatter (see "City Sanctuary", "Urban Boho", and "Above it All"). The interiors I have designed over the years for Vicki, Isabelle, Molly, and Lesli are all widely different from one another, but what all four of them have in common is an affinity for beauty and charismatic design.

opposite Bold color isn't the only way to make a statement. Though mostly neutral, the living room features a selective use of muted shades and soft textures to impart warmth and comfort. We have also brought together a stylish combination of traditional and modern design influences.

above Organic accents take their cue from natural materials.

overleaf Rustic and modern styles blend easily when united by shiplap walls painted in a soft shade of white. The large wall hanging makes an instant impression, not only because of its size but also for its gradient of gentle colors that contributes harmonious energy and a tonal balance to the scheme.

below Faithful to modern farmhouse design, the walls and the 20-foot/6-meter-high ceiling are clad in shiplap. Constructed from white oak, the floor, barstools, island, and shelves contribute to a sense of uniformity throughout the open kitchen. A rusty artifact, organic wooden bowls, and traditional earthenware pitchers add character and bring out the rustic side of farmhouse decor.

right In the dining area, a collection of matching chairs painted in a variety of colors is a playful touch that signals a "come one, come all" invitation. Soaring ceilings, white walls, and light floors create a clean backdrop that contrasts with the warm wood. The built-in banquette gives the impression that the kitchen and the porch are one and is perfectly placed to offer a view of the woods beyond.

About three years ago, Molly and Blake purchased a partially furnished home, a spacious 5,225-square-foot/ 485-square-meter farmhouse in a pastoral setting just outside Boston. It came with its own guesthouse, from which Molly runs her family's charitable foundation. The main house had lovely features such as soaring ceilings, a great layout with large rooms, and ample windows with views of the surrounding woods and fields, but it needed an infusion of the couple's own aesthetic to become truly theirs. Before they moved to Massachusetts, the Macleods had previously lived in northern California and missed many things about the area, so our goal was to bring in elements that would reflect the breezy, casual style associated with that part of the country. We also had to take the couple's environmental consciousness and design preferences into account.

below I love the enclosed porch. It's like being at the coolest nature camp but in the most comfortable way. It's also Molly and Blake's favorite spot to relax, have dinner, and entertain. We transformed the formerly cold space into an inviting spot with furniture and accessories made of wood, sheepskin, and leather. These natural materials relate to the bucolic surroundings seen through the windows, yet also maintain the interior's stylish atmosphere.

right The rugged wood of the custom table makes it the perfect companion for equally sturdy items with timeworn finishes.

"Lizzie maximized the potential of the porch in ways

we never imagined—we could not be happier
with her vision and the results."—Molly Macleod

above For the spacious entry that separates the public and private areas of the home, we used a range of neutral hues throughout for added warmth and contrast. Combining tones from the same color family helped us to keep everything grounded. The minimal decor yields a clean aesthetic that allows the few chosen items—the credenza/sideboard, leather armchairs, and rug—to shine.

Molly and Blake have discerning tastes and were very proactive, but the tricky part was to get to a place where they would both be happy with the selections of the new furnishings and accessories. I believe we achieved that, though I had to win Blake over, as he is a very pragmatic businessman, not to mention the ultimate outdoorsman. I believe all designs should be put to the test, so for me it

was a fun challenge. Molly is so appreciative when she likes something and so calm and respectful when she doesn't—working with her is a lesson in grace.

We aimed for a look that is rustic yet current and evocative of a modern Californian farmhouse: comfy, cozy, and full of welcoming charm. The goal was to strike that sweet spot between stylish and homey. One of the keys to implementing this style is to embrace the casual, rural vibe, which we realized by giving each room a neutral backdrop of white walls and light oak floors. The theme continues into the relaxed furnishings we created for them. Designing and making these custom pieces were two of the most enjoyable parts of this project and it was wonderful to see how highly Molly and Blake value quality and originality.

above The leanly furnished master bedroom takes on a spa-like quality with its uncluttered simplicity and calming palette that reflect Molly and Blake's mindful approach to living. Above the bed, the artwork by photographer Shawn Ferjanec brings home a touch of the California they love and left behind. Bedding with black accents and a bench with a woven leather seat have a sophisticated appeal, while the green plants add an organic presence.

left This peaceful bedroom corner sends out an open invitation to relax and tells a story of curated style and welcoming texture.

To help maintain a good balance, it was important to use a certain amount of restraint in selecting items so that the resulting mix would evoke low-key, laid-back luxury. We achieved this by combining old with new and high with low, as well as by incorporating natural components with a warm, slightly minimal feel.

What makes this home so inviting and liveable is its dynamic blend of finishes and materials, which we realized by layering tactile fabrics and other textural elements. The result is a sophisticated, rustic-yet-modern, and purposeful home with a fresh farmhouse feel incorporating gathering spaces that encourage all to linger and relax. But our journey has just begun, as the house has more spaces to transform. I am looking forward to continuing my work with Molly and Blake, creating thoughtfully curated rooms where they can unwind and regroup, and establishing a home that fosters a contented, authentic life.

left The master bathroom has industrial-chic accents in the form of a poured-concrete vanity and composite floor slabs. The tub is strategically positioned to take full advantage of the floor-to-ceiling windows that overlook the garden.

top A wooden plank offers a place to keep bathing necessities. The elongated shape of the tub complements the bathroom design and combines style with function.

above From rocks to plants in tactile containers, texture is a recurring theme of the decor.

Index

Page numbers in *italic* refer to the
illustrations and their captions

A

Adam Malka's house *90–109*, 91–108
Adirondack chairs *88, 118*
air plants *104*
Anaheim house *136–47*, 137–47
Archwest Developments 107

B

bar, Encino house *169*, 173
Bardot, Brigitte *131*
baskets *12, 83*
bathrooms
  Anaheim house *147*
  Boston farmhouse *201*
  California cottage *87*
  Encino house *172–3*
  Malibu beach house *109*
  Manhattan apartment *187*
batik *91*
Beck, Lawrence *176*
Beck, Rosemarie *181*
bedrooms *20*
  Adam Malka's house 99
  Anaheim house *146, 147*
  Boston farmhouse *200*
  Boston townhouse *32–3*
  California cottage *75, 86*
  Encino house *170–1*, 173
  Los Angeles apartment *117*
  Malibu beach house *108–9*
  Malibu Colony house *158–9*
  Manhattan apartment *186–9*
  Manhattan brownstone *62–3*
  Santa Monica house *42, 44–5*
  Van Buren Point cottage *130–3*, 133
Bhujodi fabrics *14, 98, 182*
Bird, Jeff and Jeannine *136–47*, 137–47
blinds *115*
Bojakijian, Mkayel 161, 168, *169*, 173
Boston farmhouse *190–201*, 191–201
Boston townhouse *22–35*, 23–35
Bryant, Barbra 6

C

California cottage *64–89*, 65–86
candles *13*
chalkboard paint *122*
Chinese Theatre, Los Angeles 111
Corvo, David *148–59*, 149–56
courtyards *see* outdoor living
Covid-19 pandemic 24, 33, 137, 139

D

Davis, Isabelle and Stephen *22–35*,
  23–35, 49, 191
decks *see* outdoor living
den, California cottage *70*
desks *see* offices
dining rooms and areas
  Adam Malka's house *92, 96*
  Anaheim house *139*
  Boston farmhouse *194–5*
  Boston townhouse *28–9*
  California cottage *69, 76–7*
  Encino house *162–3, 165, 168*
  Los Angeles apartment *114*, 117
  Malibu beach house *103–5*, 108
  Malibu Colony house *152*
  Manhattan apartment *182–3*
  Santa Monica house *40–1*
  Van Buren Point cottage *123–7*
displays, California cottage *73–4, 79*
Dunkirk 119

E

Eames, Charles 31, *51*
Egyptian Theatre, Los Angeles 111
Elle Decor 50
Encino house *160–75*, 161–74
Erie, Lake 119
Everhart, Tom *132*

F

family rooms
  Anaheim house *140–1*
  Boston townhouse *26–7*, 33
Ferjanec, Shawn *110–17*, 111–17, *200*
fireplaces
  Boston townhouse *28*
  California cottage *87*
  Malibu beach house *109*

Manhattan brownstone *55, 60*
  Santa Monica house *36*
  Van Buren Point cottage *123*, 133
floors, stencilled *50, 88*
focal points *21*
foyers
  Adam Malka's house *90*
  Encino house *166–9*
  see also hallways

G

gardens *see* outdoor living
Glatter, Lesli Linka *176–89*, 177–85, 191
Gordon, Vicki 23, *49–62*, 48–63, *177*, 191
GQ magazine 18
Grauman, Sid 111
guesthouse, California cottage *82–6*,
  86

H

hallways
  Anaheim house *142*
  Boston farmhouse *198–9*
  Boston townhouse *25*
  California cottage *72*
  Manhattan apartment 180
  Manhattan brownstone *58*
  see also foyers
Hernandez, Eloy *88*
Hollywood style 111–15

I

India *14, 98*
Inglewood, Los Angeles 65

K

Kilbane, John 107
kitchens
  Adam Malka's house *92–3*
  Anaheim house *144–5*
  Boston farmhouse *194–5*
  Boston townhouse *30–1*
  California cottage *71*
  Los Angeles apartment *115*, 117
  Malibu beach house *106–7*, 108
  Malibu Colony house *152*
  Manhattan apartment *184–5*
  Manhattan brownstone *54–7*
  Santa Monica house *40*
  Van Buren Point cottage *128–9*

L
landing, Adam Malka's house *98*
Levine, Heather *117*
library, Manhattan brownstone 59, *61*
living rooms *17*
    Adam Malka's house *92–5*
    Anaheim house *136–8*
    Boston farmhouse *192–3*
    Boston townhouse *22–4*, 31
    California cottage *66–7*, *85*
    Encino house *164–5*, 168
    Los Angeles apartment *110–13*, 117
    Malibu beach house *104–5*, 108
    Malibu Colony house *148*, *150–1*
    Manhattan apartment *178–81*, 180
    Manhattan brownstone *48–52*
    Santa Monica house *36–9*
    Van Buren Point cottage *120–2*
Los Angeles 18, 65
Los Angeles apartment *110–17*, *111–17*

M
McGraw, William J 9, 68, *88*, 119
Macleod, Molly and Blake *190–201*,
    191–201
Malibu beach house *100–9*, *101–8*
Malibu Colony house *148–59*, *149–56*
Malka, Adam *90–109*, *91–108*
Manhattan apartment *176–89*, *177–85*
Manhattan brownstone *48–63*, *49–63*
Marine, Joni and Jeff *100–9*, *101–8*
Mediterranean architecture 137
Meier, Richard 119
Meyer & Holler 111
Morocco
    pillows 23
    rugs *39*, *60*, *90*, *95*, *97*, *189*
mudcloth *93*
Muscle Shoals Sound Studio *169*, 173

N
New York City 18
    Manhattan apartment *176–89*, *177–85*
    Manhattan brownstone *48–63*,
    49–63
New York State cottage *118–35*, *119–34*
Noguchi, Isamu 24, *39*, *41*, *42*
nursery
    Boston townhouse *34–5*

O
offices
    Encino house 168, *174–5*
    Malibu Colony house *153*
    Santa Monica house *43*
O'Keefe and Merritt stoves *71*
Old Hollywood style *111–15*
outdoor living
    Adam Malka's house *97*
    California cottage *78–81*, *88–9*
    Santa Monica house *46–7*
    Van Buren Point cottage *118*

P
Pacific Ocean 39, *107*, *108*, 153, 156
pantry, Manhattan brownstone *55*
Pardini, Laura *110–17*, *111–17*
Parson, Brainard *130*
Pearsall, Adrian *181*
peg racks *68*
Pei, I.M. 119
pillows *13*, *23*, *86*, *91*, 117
plants *83*
porches
    Boston farmhouse *196–7*
    California cottage *64–5*
    Van Buren Point cottage *134–5*
powder rooms
    Anaheim house *143*
    Santa Monica house *45*

R
Ray, Rex *113*
recycling *76*
Roberts, Julia 13
Roubinet, Julien 25
Rubin, Michael 23, 50, 62

S
Saarinen, Eero *28*
Santa Monica house *36–47*, *37–44*
scarves *12*
shutters *53*, *73*
Spanish Revival style 137
staircases
    Adam Malka's house *90*, *98*
    Encino house *167–8*
    Malibu Colony house *148*, *150*
stencilling 50, *88*, *114*, 117
Stern, Dan and Nanna *36–47*, *37–44*
straw hats *12*
striped textiles *18*

sunroom
    Malibu Colony house 153–4, *154–5*
suzani fabric *115*
swimming pool, Malibu beach house
    100, *102*

T
Tafipolsky, Semion *137–9*
terraces *see* outdoor living
Thailand 63
"theater", Malibu Colony house *156–7*
Tischker, Beka and Ben *160–75*, *161–74*
Tumbleweed & Dandelion *8–21*, *9–18*,
    33, 161
Twain, Mark 120

V
Van Buren Point cottage *118–35*, *119–34*
Venice Beach, California 9, 18, 65
Vidal, Gore 84

W
Weinrib, Madeline 31
West Africa 63
Willens, Michele *148–59*, *149–56*

Acknowledgements

Many people have helped to provide the opportunity to write this book. First and foremost, I owe this honor to Fifi O'Neill – without her, there was only an idea. Thanks also to Mark Lohman for his wit and photography, and to the team at CICO Books: Cindy Richards, who commissioned this book, Sophie Devlin, who edited it, Louise Leffler, for her design, Sally Powell, for art direction, and the production and sales and publicity teams.

Thank you to my crew. This includes my friends (all of whom are expecting credit), and my family (all of whom deserve credit), and my Tumbleweed & Dandelion team. (all of whom supported me to the finish line).

William J McGraw and Virginia K McGraw: You allowed me to create my own world when I was young so I could thrive in the real world when I became less young. Thank you Eunice Matilda Wuerstle for the driving lessons and Aunt Dottie for inventing shorts. To Barbra Bryant for everything.

And to Joe Bifaro, for picking up the pieces and showing us how to behave in your eighties.

Thank you Sean Patrick McGraw and Dr. Colleen K McGraw (I win for best siblings), Deb McGraw, Jon Hall McGraw, Christine Cockerham, Suzanne Walker, Mkayel Bojakijian, Tatiana Tomicki, Hilary Romaine, Amanda Dugan, Eloy Hernandez, Vitaly, Gillian Schoenfeld, Genie Covarrubias, Courtney Delancey, Christie Merritt, Ruth De Jong, Brian O'Connor, Merlin, Gio, Max, Alfredo #1 and #2, Connie Ortega, Whitney Leigh Morris, and Adam Chardis, without whom there would not have been the idea that started this.

Finally, thank you to Victoria Gordon, for always lifting me up and having friends whose houses I can play in, and to all of my dear clients and friends for agreeing to be a part of this journey. And, most importantly, to Jonathan Mark Fineman, for being the man that appreciates me, even when I am just being me.